D1162552

JOHN WESLEY

INGVAR HADDAL

JOHN WESLEY

A Biography

translated from the original NORWEGIAN

ABINGDON PRESS
NEW YORK . NASHVILLE

SET IN MONOTYPE PLANTIN AND PRINTED IN
GREAT BRITAIN BY THE CAMELOT PRESS LTD
LONDON AND SOUTHAMPTON

Contents

Foreword

New books are continually being written about John Wesley. Like no other figure of the eighteenth century he excites the interest of both scholars and general readers curious to know more about the founder of Methodism.

What was he like? The present book is no learned treatise on either Wesley or his work. Nor is it a disparaging psychological analysis. I will merely endeavour to relate quite plainly the various situations Wesley encountered and how he reacted to them. Then each of us will be able to decide for himself 'what he was like'.

I have not tried to present any glossy picture of him. He himself would have liked that least of all. But after studying him in my leisure hours over a number of years I can only say: God grant our age, too, a man like John Wesley—a man who could unite in himself intelligence, industry, poetic gifts, talent for organization, a complete lack of fear of his fellow men combined with an absolute fear of God in the same remarkable degree!

This book is based on a study of Wesley's journals, letters, hymns, sermons, and various other writings, as well as on Charles Wesley's journal and a number of old and new biographies of Wesley.

INGVAR HADDAL

Chapter I

The Rector of Epworth

THE RECTOR had not properly accustomed himself to his new surroundings yet. And there were practically no limits to what a servant of the Church might meet in the year 1705! When the door had crashed to behind him an hour ago it was almost like waking from a bad dream to a still worse reality. He, Samuel Wesley, descendant of an old English aristocratic line, had landed in a debtors' jail! Thus far had things gone with him.

He looked at the pitiful creatures who were to be his fellow prisoners for no one knew how long. Many of them had seen better days. There, for example, was an old officer trying to conceal under his military coat the bitter fact that even his watch and chain were lodged with the pawnbroker. And there was an old merchant he knew. He, too, was trying to preserve his dignity, but his clothes showed clearly that all his former splendour was now irrevocably past.

Here was teeming life, men and women, young and old. Flocks of children had followed their parents into misfortune. Here were to be found scoundrels and cheats, former officials and people of substance, gamblers and drunkards, and many like Samuel Wesley himself who had merely been unfortunate in the great game of life. It was like a cross-section of the Old England which was just then moaning under that protracted and painful process of social readjustment which is called the Industrial Revolution. After a while most of them took it all lightly and humorously. One gets used to so much in life, and the long struggle against poverty had made most of them confident that such things would one day pass. The days went by in one way or another. The prisoners visited each other in their rooms and sought to keep up appearances by a form of despairing, indigent gentility and punctiliousness about titles and forms.

But one pleasure they could not deny themselves, and that was the pleasure of welcoming new arrivals with undisguised malevolence. Here at the entrance to Lincoln Castle there was indeed variety and diversion enough, as for instance today, when the little rector of Epworth was cast inside, red in the face with anger, swinging his arms and protesting loudly against his treatment.

A contented grin adorned the face of Lincoln Jail when the news of Samuel Wesley's imprisonment spread among the prisoners. Now they would have the opportunity of tormenting this detested scourger of souls! But those who knew him best, those from his own parish, did not believe that anyone would get much happiness out of that, for they knew their shepherd, and feared and respected him, even though in many cases these feelings took the form of a primitive hate.

Who did not recall how he had banished people from the communion-table for committing some trifling misdemeanour or other? What shame fell upon those to whom it happened! They could not even take the sacrament the three times a year prescribed. And had he not made very minor sinners stand on the cold floor of the church in their bare feet Sunday after Sunday in the hope of inducing them to be more contrite? But it was not contrition that followed. They tried to ruin him in every way they could. They stabbed and hurt his cows. They uprooted his flax crops or set them on fire. And they called after his children so that he himself would hear: 'Be off with you, you devil's brats. We'll soon have you out begging.'

His good parishioners had always been stiff-necked. When the King was proposing to drain their marshy land and make it fertile soil, he had had to fight in order to carry it through. And once, too, the rabble, in a frenzy, had broken into the church and smashed the tablets bearing the inscription of God's Ten Commandments.

Could it be that he did not suit Epworth? His congregation was interested in pig-breeding and farm-management and fox-hunting. And if there was anything Samuel Wesley was not interested in it was practical affairs. Master Samuel preferred to be a poet. He styled himself the 'Island Poet of Axholme', even if the 'island' he lived on was only a bit of Old England surrounded by rivers and canals.

And now it seemed that he who had his head full of beautiful poems, and who even had a certain output of his own behind him, was to starve in insanitary quarters, financially distressed, hated by dissenters and barbarians. The higher he tried to soar on poetry's wings, the deeper he sank into poverty's black mire, until finally he had landed in the debtors' jail.

No, Master Samuel was not interested in practical matters and he had never been able to make the parsonage pay for itself. This was undeniably sad, considering that Susanna his wife, or Sukey as he called her, provided him with a new mouth to fill almost every single year.

His stipend, it is true, was not the lowest possible. When he began as a curate in London in 1688 he received £28 a year. Later he went to South Ormsby as Rector, where he lived in a miserable little hovel, with a stipend of £50 a year. And then finally he had come to Epworth, the reward for a poem he had written to the Queen. He had, perhaps, hoped that by dedicating all his poems to the royal house he would have been given a diocese in Ireland, but it was only to be Epworth this time. The stipend here was £50 a year.

That was not enough, and so he had had to start borrowing money to keep going, with the result that his total debts now amounted to some £300. Nevertheless, what had brought him to his present straits was merely a rag of a debt of £30.

It had been no small shock for him to come out of church on that day after a christening and be met by Mr Pinder standing on the steps and waving his note of hand under his nose. Would he kindly pay not only the interest which was due, but the whole amount, altogether in an hour! The Rector had answered that naturally he hadn't that much money by him at the moment, but that he would try to secure it, sell the furniture or the live-stock or whatever might be necessary. He would, of course, have to have a few days' or at least a few hours' notice. For a while it had seemed that Pinder would agree to this, but some of those Dissenter devils were present and they took Pinder by the sleeve and sprayed the poisonous idea into his ear that there was only one thing to be done, to take him to prison in the nearest town, that is, Lincoln.

Thus it was, then, that he had arrived in this miserable cell. Everywhere was filthy and disgusting. True, he was never in danger. Susanna had sent him her wedding-ring, a brooch and a golden chain. These could be converted into money so that he could buy food. But this he would not do. He entertained gallant thoughts of returning it all to Susanna the moment he got out. There was probably something needed at home, too. He had no idea whether there was any food in the house, for he never took any interest in such things, but he knew that Susanna would find some way out.

Just now, though, he preferred to think of something pleasant. He would sit down here on the stool and dream about something which would make him forget his difficulties, or at least give him courage and fortitude. The Island Poet would let the rustling of the old family tree soothe his soul. He would let the faces in the portrait gallery of his ancestors nod down at him. 'Great is the heritage of the man born of good family.'

His great-grandfather, and therefore his children's great-great-grandfather, was called Herbert Westley and came from Westleigh in Devonshire. He bore a title and was called Sir Herbert, and he married a lady who was also of the nobility, Elisabeth de Wellesley. Samuel Wesley didn't know very much about these ancestors of his, but nevertheless, it was after them that he had named his children.

Herbert's son was called Bartholomew Westley. He had studied theology and medicine at the University of Oxford, the first of four generations of Wesleys to be educated there. He, too, had married a lady of the aristocracy, in 1619. In his maturity he became parish parson in Catherstone on the south coast of England. He was very short in stature, like all the family, and for this reason was nicknamed 'The Puny Parson'.

It is said of this clergyman that he was loved and respected by the people of the neighbourhood and that he lived a very pious life. The following story is told of his habits of prayer.

There was political unrest in the country, and the power of the High Church Stuart kings with their inclination towards Catholicism was tottering before the lords of Parliament. The struggle occupied the minds of everybody, and in the South there was little sympathy for the King, Charles II. Then one dark night in 1651 a strange company of travellers came to the town. No one knew who they were, but curiosity was aroused when they sat up the whole night in the tavern without going to rest, and continually kept sending someone down to the coast, as if they were on the look-out for a boat. Soon a rumour began to spread that it was the King fleeing the country. Now the people would willingly have arrested the King, but dared not without consulting the parson who was considered an important figure among them. But the parson was at this moment saying his prayers and no one dared to disturb him. And Pastor Bartholomew's prayers lasted a very long time, so long, in fact, that when he had finally finished in the early hours of the morning, the bird had flown. 'Yes,' said the little parson, 'methinks that if the King ever returns to England he will be fond of long prayers, for had my prayer been shorter this evening, we should have taken him.'

King Charles did return, and the year 1662 was a year of trial and adversity for the English clergy. Many of them lost their positions and were thrown into jail for refusing to discharge their divine services as the King dictated in accordance with the official Prayer Book. The little parson lost his position, too, though no one dared to do him any harm because he was so well loved by the people of the neighbourhood. He survived only eight years longer, and during this time practised as a doctor.

Samuel's father was called John Westley. From him the great founder of Methodism was to inherit both his name and many of his traits of character. John Westley was born in the year 1636, and was educated at Oxford, where he studied Oriental languages. He kept a detailed diary in which he noted down his thoughts and feelings as well as his outward experiences. He visited men in prison, made plans to travel to America as a missionary, and all his days led a wandering life as a parson. He is a sort of model for the grandson with the same name whom he was never destined to see. He too, was a God-fearing and diligent winner of souls. The year 1662 meant for him, too, the loss of his position, and later he was imprisoned no less than four times for his defiance and his convictions. During the last years of his life he was a well-loved and very zealous Dissenter parson, until he was released from poverty and adversity by a merciful death in the year 1678.

These, then, were the men who nodded down encouragingly to Samuel as he sat in his cell in Lincoln Jail in 1705.

Samuel could not forbear not smiling. His sense of humour had deserted him: the atmosphere of a prison was no new thing for the Wesley family. His father had sat there four times. For him it was only the first time. His father and grandfather had finished up as Dissenting ministers and the intention was that he should be one also. He had attended Dissenting schools until he was fifteen when he had gone to London to attend a Dissenting academy. There he had begun to write poetry and had had it published, and a eulogistic review had founded in him a poetic ambition which never disappeared.

At the academy he had been given the exercise of writing a tract against the Church. He had gone conscientiously to work and immersed himself in very detailed preliminary studies—and arrived at the conclusion that the Church was right and he and the Dissenters wrong. Samuel Wesley was never the man to permit time to elapse between thought and action and it was not long before he broke away from the academy and with four shillings in his pocket betook himself to Oxford. Here he had struggled through by polishing shoes, sweeping floors, and writing exercises and essays for the lazy sons of wealthy parents who employed their time in quite different pursuits. Finally, ordained deacon in 1688 by the Bishop of Rochester at his palace at Bromley and ordained priest in 1689 at St Andrew's, Holborn, the transformation was complete. The son of a Dissenter had broken with his past to become a High Churchman.

In order to prove to himself and to others just how zealous he was on behalf of the High Church, he had attacked, in the manner of the age, his former friends among the Dissenters and disclosed flaws and sins he had got to know about through his intimate connection with the Dissenting schools and his old school-friend Daniel Defoe, the journalist who later wrote the book about the adventures of Robinson Crusoe. Samuel Wesley and Daniel Defoe broke many a lance in this connexion.

The Dissenters remained his great enemies throughout his life, together with Satan, the world, and his own flesh. Taken all in all his great zeal for his own Church brought him many difficulties and opponents. Worst of all was the fact that only with difficulty could he control his own temper.

But on one occasion, at least, his violent and fearless temperament had saved a soul.

He was sitting in a coffee-house, few others near him, and one of these, an officer, kept on swearing continually and with deep emphasis.

Samuel asked the serving girl for a glass of water, and when it arrived requested her to carry it to that gentleman in the red coat, and desire him to wash his mouth after his oaths. The infuriated colonel tried to seize Wesley, but the others intervened and told him that it might well have been for his good to do his swearing in the presence of a parson.

But the story did not end there. Many years later Samuel Wesley was sitting in St James's Park in London. Suddenly a stranger came over to him and said: 'I recognize you, and I am happy to meet you again. Since that time, sire, I thank God, I have feared an oath, and everything that is offensive to the divine Majesty; and as I have a perfect recollection of you, I rejoiced at seeing you, and could not refrain from expressing my gratitude to God and you.'

The prisoners who had thought that they would scarcely get any great pleasure out of having Samuel Wesley in the prison turned out to be right. His gloomy brooding and contemplation lasted no longer than two days. Then he threw off his troubles with a jerk, and began to exercise his stern ministrations upon the souls of his fellow-prisoners. He spoke with each one individually about his faith and intentions, he questioned and catechized and examined the state of the prisoners' Christian knowledge. This he found far from satisfactory, and forthwith wrote to 'The Society for Promoting Christian Knowledge' for religious tracts to hand round. In every detail he showed himself the same zealous servant of the Church as he had always been.

On Sundays he held divine service and no one might absent himself: the prison warders gathered the prisoners together and they had no choice but to listen.

The Rector shone at this period, happy at the size of the gathering he now had to address. He blossomed into pleasantry in a letter to his Archbishop, telling this powerful man who was also a member of the Privy Council that now he had finally come to rest, now his vessel had reached the port for which it had so long been bound. He told his superior the size of his debt and begged him not to think less of him because his address was no longer the rectory at Epworth but the prison at Lincoln.

Samuel Wesley was a diligent clergyman and a sincere Christian. Unfortunately his ardour was not always attended by the necessary discrimination. His literary output was large, but the quality stood in inverse proportion to the quantity.

John Wesley inherited his father's industry and pronounced enterprise even in the face of difficulties. But apart from this, he was not greatly influenced by the example of his father. From his father's line he inherited a strong and independent character and an ardent interest in the Kingdom of God. From his father's line, too, he inherited a lifelong interest in medicine. John's great-grandfather, as has been said, was a doctor as well as a clergyman, and his Uncle Matthew, Samuel's brother, was a much consulted doctor in London. In the healing of the body John Wesley was in advance of his time, but his greatest work lay in the healing of the soul.

Chapter II

Susanna

SOMEONE WAS knocking at the door of the old rectory in Epworth. The maid went to open the door, but in the schoolroom work continued as if nothing had happened, for that was how Susanna liked it. Only wild little Hetty was unable to restrain herself and felt a desire to look out of the window. But one glance from her mother sufficed to bring her head back to her lessons again and she carried on from where she had stopped.

But now the maid entered. The children looked up from their lessons with surprise and curiosity registered on their faces. It was something quite unheard of that servants should come in and interrupt while they were busy with their lessons or when Mistress Susanna was teaching the children.

It could only mean that something quite out of the ordinary was happening. And indeed it was. There outside stood an array of carriages and fine horses which had all the appearance of having come from a great distance. The maid was so flurried by the magnificence of the visit that she was scarcely able to stammer out the name of the person standing outside. It was no less than the Archbishop of York himself, asking whether the lady of the house was at home to callers. Never before had the maid been called upon to admit so important a personage.

Nor for that matter had Mistress Susanna, but it would have required more than that to put her out of countenance. If there was anything wrong, it could hardly be worse than what had happened already, her husband in a debtors' jail and practically no food in the house. And if the Archbishop was there for any good reason, then there was surely nothing to be anxious about. In a flash the children were packed off upstairs with their slates and books, with instructions to carry on with their reading until they had learnt the day's lessons—and the room was now ready for the reception of the distinguished guest.

Archbishop Sharp was a very lovable man who had left his favourite occupation, the study of old coins, in order to come to the help of his subordinate in his trials. He surveyed the room, small but well-kept and clean. But it is as though extreme poverty is shrieking a greeting at him from every corner. The Archbishop is moved to his inmost soul.

But soon the room was forgotten, for the little woman who now approached him attracted the whole of his attention to herself. A long life had taught the Archbishop to be a judge of character, and he soon saw that he was standing in the presence of a personality the like of which one does not find every day. Pretty in the true sense of the word she was not, but she did possess a fine, agile figure and a good carriage, managing to combine a dignified posture with a humble and modest manner. Her hair was dark brown and plentiful, her eyes imperious but kind.

But as they conversed together he became deeply impressed. He realized that he was a facing a woman who would bear the blows of life without a murmur and without becoming bitter and hard. He observed too, how God-fearing she was and how fervent her desire to be of service to the Church. Furthermore, she was able to discuss doctrinal matters and literature in a manner that would have excited the envy of many a clergyman. About politics, too, she had her own very firm views. Nothing, it seemed, was beyond the capabilities of this woman.

At the same time the Archbishop was distressed by the circumstances that life had brought to this richly endowed lady. It was therefore with all the more happiness that he was able to inform Mistress Susanna that her days of affliction would soon be at an end. He himself would arrange for half of her husband's debt to be paid at once, and what remained he would get written off. Indeed, he could even announce that Her Majesty the Queen had been pleased to interest herself in the affair and that they were to benefit from her generosity.

'Tell me, Mrs Wesley, whether you ever really wanted bread,' said the Archbishop.

Susanna's answer is classical in its candour:

'My lord, I will freely own to your Grace that, strictly speaking, I never did want bread. But then, I had so much care to get it before it was eat, and to pay for it after, as has often made it very unpleasant to me. And I think to have bread on such terms is the next degree of wretchedness to having none at all.'

A sum of money was left lying on the table when the Archbishop left. Mistress Susanna thanked him courteously. She said she understood the happiness his Grace must have had in making the gift, and her own happiness in accepting it was no less: she hoped he would see in her heartfelt contentment a sufficient reward for the trouble he had taken on their behalf.

Susanna Wesley was the daughter of one of England's outstanding Dissenting preachers, Doctor Samuel Annesley. He, too, had been a minister in the Established Church until the year 1662. But in mind and heart he was a Puritan, and the famous Act of Uniformity had forced him to retire from Church and office, like Bartholomew and John Westley, when he could not bring himself to swear to order his services according to the official Prayer Book.

Susanna always thought about her home in Spital Yard with the greatest thankfulness. Even if she and her family had come to be on different sides in the religious issue—she as a member of the Church and the others as Dissenters—it was nevertheless there that she had been grounded in her puritanical and strict way of life. She was grateful for the education she had been given at home. It was a wonderful legacy to take out with one into life.

Nevertheless, this was the only legacy she had had. Her father, like all his colleagues, was a poor man. He did, however, possess a certain streak of humour. This was revealed, for instance, after his decease, when the family assembled to open his will. They all knew that there would not be a great deal to divide. But all the same a slight smile flitted across their sorrow when the following words were read out:

'Of what I shall leave behind me, I make this short disposal,—My just debts being paid, I give to each of my children one shilling, and all the rest to be equally divided between my son Benjamin Annesley, my daughter Judith Annesley, and my daughter Ann Annesley, whom I make my Executors of this my last Will and Testament; revoking all former, and confirming this with my hand and seal this 29 of March, 1693.'

So Susanna took but one shilling with her when she left home. It was to prove to be a lucky shilling.

Even if Dr Annesley had been able to give to most of his children only a single shilling, it was, nevertheless, no mean disbursement, for his children were many. Susanna was the very youngest of a flock of brothers and sisters totalling twenty-four or twenty-five—historians have never been quite sure of the exact figure.

At that time a family containing so many children must evidently have been a matter of little moment, for when Susanna was baptized by Pastor Thomas Manton, he was asked how many children Dr Annesley actually had.

'Two dozen, I believe, or a quarter of a hundred,' he answered. 'The reckoning children by dozens is a singular circumstance,—an honour to which few persons ever arrive.'

It was here in her childhood home that she had decided that she would never spend more time on pleasure than on prayer. This promise she had made to herself as a young girl and she had kept it ever since.

But what was it, incidentally, that she had meant by 'pleasure'? Well, in the first place there were her anthologies of poetry, heavy poems, filled, as the manner of the age was, with figures from Roman and Greek mythology, in which it was necessary to be well versed if one was so much as to understand, let alone enjoy, them. Then there were the discussions in the parsonage. These turned mostly on religious matters, on the relationship between the Church and the Dissenters, and on difficult theological and philosophical problems. That is what she meant by pleasure.

Eagerly she had plunged into the talks, and even though she was still a girl, her opinions were attentively heard. And when she had thought about the question of the Dissenters and the Church and independently arrived at the conclusion that the Church was right and the Dissenters wrong, she had confronted her father and said so.

It gave Dr Annesley no joy to permit his daughter to enter the Established Church. After all, it was the enemy he had fought ever since 1662. But when he saw how determined she was and how she could put forward reasons for her point of view, he realized that this was no young girl's foolish notion, but a resolute decision. The parson knew his daughter well, and knew that if she had once decided upon a course of action after long deliberation, then sooner or later it would be put into effect.

Susanna also, however, looked back upon that period in her childhood home with a certain horror. Many of those who were Dissenters at that time joined the Unitarians, who denied the Trinity. There was only one God, they said, namely the Father in Heaven. It was Him Jesus Christ had come to tell us about. But Jesus Himself was no god, only a teacher, a prophet. This doctrine was fascinating to the mind, and it attracted Susanna's logical sense not a little.

It was at this time that she met a young man from Exeter College in Oxford. He was, like herself, the child of a Dissenter who had fallen in love with the national Church. But he was stronger in his faith than she was. She remembered him as a zealous, glowing, young man, small in stature, with fine features and a cultured appearance. With what enthusiasm the two pursued their religious studies in those happy early days! It was as if the difficult theological problems were inexhaustible when the two sat together discussing them hour after hour. He spoke in his customary glowing way, and she would answer quietly and reflectively.

After the lapse of a certain time Susanna knew that this young student would one day win her for the old orthodox Church. And what was more, he would one day win her for himself, too. Susanna had experienced that which her lavender-perfumed poetry album talked about in ambiguous terms. Susanna had known what it was to be in love.

Still she loved this man. But when now she looked back on that period of her life, she was all the more thankful that he had chosen her for her true faith rather than for herself. For life with Samuel

Wesley had not always been a bed of roses. But how would it have gone with her soul if she had denied faith in Christ the true God?

Indeed, so grateful was she to him in the matter of faith that when Samuel died in 1735, she rejected the verse suggested by her poet son as an inscription for his grave. Instead she composed the inscription herself, and chiselled in the stone by unskilled hands there were the words:

Here
Lieth all that was Mortal
of Samuel Wesley, A.M. He was
Rector of Epworth 39 years
and departed this Life 25 of
April 1735 Aged 72.
As he liv'd so he died in the
true Catholic Faith of the
Holy Trinity in unity and
that Jesus Christ is God
incarnate and the only Saviour
of mankind.

This inscription, since re-cut by a skilled mason, testifies as much to the person who wrote it as to the person for whom it was written.

In 1688 they had married and gone off to a small living in South Ormsby where they lived in the little rectory. In all essentials this had been a happy time. Her husband had continued to write poetry to her. Here, too, she had experienced the miracle of feeling a new life move beneath her heart. It had been a period of consecration for her. She had gone there to battle in the company of God, and she vowed that if her child were a boy, he would be dedicated to God as a servant in His temple. She felt herself identified with all those other saintly women of old who had been through the same fight. A boy it was, and he was christened Samuel after his father and after the great servant of the temple in the Old Testament. He was dedicated to the ministry even before he was born. But it was not so with her other two boys, John and Charles. They were allowed to choose for themselves.

Even if Susanna was aware that she had powers and abilities within her, she still had to devote herself for the most part to her home, her husband, and her children. Her relations with her husband were not always easy. Life was to become one long struggle for them both, for strong and determined were the wills that had to be mastered. For the most part things went well enough, but occasional eruptions were not quite unknown.

For Susanna according to the word of the Bible had to be submissive to her husband. She called him her master and would like to have lived according to the beliefs of her ancestors. But later in life writing to her son John she says how unfortunate it was that she and her husband should never have thought alike about everything. In addition he was extremely quick-tempered and ambitious, as many small people are.

This mood he vented mostly on the Dissenters, lacking as they now seemed to be in much of their early ardour and sacrificial zeal. But he vented it on her, too, and even though she had every desire to be submissive to her husband, she nevertheless, had quite definite views on how far this submissiveness should go. She would never, for example, permit her husband to decide what sort of political opinions she should hold. She would reserve that privilege for herself. Her husband was accustomed to say an evening prayer for King William of Orange. Well, he was entitled to do so if he wished, that was his own affair. But she would never even say so much as Amen to such a prayer, for she herself prayed in her heart for the Stuarts, who in her opinion were the rightful heirs to the English throne, by virtue of God and the law. Nor did it matter to her if her husband, bright red with temper, stopped praying and asked why she didn't say Amen to his prayer. It was not even a matter of crucial importance if he in a fury packed a few clothes and set off for London with the Parthian shaft: 'You and I must part: for if we have two kings, we must have two beds.'

She kept silent because she thought she was in the right. Of course he returned a year later, in 1702, when the Stuart Queen Anne was placed on the throne. It was in this happy reconciliation period that John was born, on 17th June 1703. Already when she was expecting him Susanna knew that God intended him for some special purpose. It was a happy time for both husband and wife. Peace and harmony reigned throughout the home. Her husband had become manageable. The next daughter to arrive was given the Stuart name Anne, and the last son to see the light of day was christened Charles, another Stuart name.

Susanna brought up and educated her children herself. Because of the size of her family she made a virtue of necessity and introduced a fixed plan and method into their upbringing. Susanna herself realized it was strict, but she thought it better for them to learn obedience at home than outside. Mothers who permitted their children to grow up in their own way she called cruel.

Her children were whipped from the age of one if they misbehaved themselves. And then they were expected to 'cry softly'. How else would one get a moment's peace with this great flock of children? The whole system depended upon breaking the child's will while it was still small, so that it would be easier for the grown-ups to direct it until the time came that it was mature enough to decide things for itself.

For her eldest son, Samuel, she had once had a tutor, 'whose goodness Samuel could tell from his protruding knuckles'. But he was a drunkard and was dismissed, and Susanna was able to start shaping the future Methodists herself.

The family observed a certain code of honour. If a present was once given, it must not be taken back. The children were not permitted to address even one another by name alone, but were required to say 'Sister Sukey' or 'Brother Samuel'. If anyone committed an offence it was Susanna's rule that they should escape punishment if they confessed. 'This rule prevented a good deal of lying,' she recalls later in a letter to John when he had questioned her about her educational methods, and added (referring to the Rector): 'and would have done more if one in the family would have observed it.' She doubtless had difficulty in trying to reduce her husband to her strict system.

They were allowed no food between meals and had to take the food that was offered them even though they did not like it. Nor was it permitted to reach out for food. They must wait until they were given more or else quietly whisper their desires to one of the servant girls who would then carry their requests to Susanna in person. Going out into the street to play with all types of children was also strictly forbidden. After all they might find out about things which in Susanna's opinion should be reserved for grown-ups.

Under no circumstances were the children permitted to have any lessons until they had reached their fifth year, but the day after their fifth birthday their formal education began. They attended classes for six hours and on the very first day they were supposed to learn the whole of the alphabet. All her children except two managed this feat, and these seemed to Susanna to be very backward. Later when she compared them with other children she had reason to revise this opinion. The second day of school was if possible even more solemn, for then the Bible was brought out and they were permitted to begin spelling through the first verse, 'In the beginning God created . . .'. This did not always go well at the start, but no other lesson was begun until they could manage it. Before the end of morning school they were required to review everything they had learnt that day, and before evening prayers the work set for the afternoon also had to be run through and repeated.

Her choleric husband exclaimed at the perseverance which made her tell a child the same thing twenty times. 'Had I satisfied myself by mentioning the matter only nineteen times, I should have lost all my labour,' she replied. 'You see it was the twentieth time that crowned the whole.'

The children got a good education. Daughters included, they all learnt Latin and Greek and were well tutored in the classical studies that were traditional in England at that time.

But more important to Susanna than learning was to ingraft upon her children while they were still young the fear of God, 'the principles of the true religion', as she called it. It was therefore most natural for John to turn to his mother later in his studies, not only in practical, everyday issues, but also in theological matters, even including the question of his own peace of mind.

It may well be that Susanna sinned against many of the rules set up in modern times for the education of children. And it is also possible that she reared children as much for eternity as for her own day. But it is precisely because she set her stamp so deeply on her son John and instilled such good habits in him that she has with the greatest justification been called 'The Mother of Methodism'.

Chapter III

At the Old Rectory

After three months' imprisonment in the debtors' jail Samuel Wesley returned to his parish, and life was able to continue as before. The Rector still snorted with rage over the Dissenters and disciplined his own congregation with a hard hand. As before, he went from house to house and visited the people in their homes, and not a single one of them was permitted to escape his talks on religious matters.

Antagonism towards him smouldered in Epworth as never before. While he had been sitting in jail his cows had been injured. On election day the rabble had gathered about the parsonage and made a noise until far into the night, so that it was impossible to get to sleep. When the maid finally did fall asleep in the early hours of the morning she happened to lie on top of the youngest member of the family without noticing it and the little thing was suffocated.

The Bishop had offered to transfer Samuel to another parish where the people were more co-operative than these half-barbarian parishioners of his. But Samuel would not hear of it. He still believed he could do some good in Epworth and preferred to remain.

Now that he had thrown off the heavy burden of his debt, he could get on with a work that had occupied his thoughts for a long time, a treatise on the theme of Job. It was going to be written in Latin with the title *Dissertationes in Librum Jobi* (*Dissertations on the Book of Job*). It was going to be the greatest work of his life and might, perhaps, provide something for the ever empty family coffer. Right up to the day of his death Wesley worked on this book and he became so absorbed in it that the popularity of the other members of the family depended upon how they were disposed towards this old, sorely-tried man of suffering. Job became in effect a new member of Wesley's family, and several of Wesley's children and children-in-law were co-opted to help with the book.

Young Samuel had gone off to a boarding-school in London. Some of the children were dead, but there were still eight living at home in the rectory. Susanna was expecting her nineteenth and last child in March 1709. She now received valuable assistance from her eldest daughters who were almost grown-up.

The rectory was 'built all of timber and plaister', with three storys and seven rooms. The living-room was on the ground floor and the bedrooms and the Rector's study on the first floor. The roof was thatched.

It was cold and dark when the parson's family retired on the night of the 8th February 1709. But outside there was someone skulking about hidden by the mist and darkness.

Little Jackie was awakened by the light in his room. He thought it was morning already and remained lying in bed a little longer waiting for the maid to come and fetch him as she usually did. But no girl came. That was strange. Things always happened punctually in Susanna's house. Perhaps he should try calling? He mustn't be too far behind the others.

He shouted, but no one came. He shouted again. Still no girl. On the other hand, however, he could hear some hallooing and shouting going on outside. This would have to be investigated. True he had been ordered always to remain in bed until the maid came to fetch him, but surely this was an exception which would, perhaps, permit a deviation from Mother's strict rules.

Could it be Father's enemies making a noise outside like they did on election day? Was somebody trying to harm them? Well, he'd soon find out if he went down and looked into the matter.

John scrambled out of bed on his little five-year-old legs and opened the door leading down to the staircase. Then something strange happened: he was struck by a fearful heat and smoke and flames came rolling into the room and set alight the ceiling above him. It was clearly not possible to go down that way. But there was no other way. He crawled across to the window, up on to the little chest that stood there.

There he saw a strange and terrible sight, almost like what he had imagined Hell must be.

It could not have been long past midnight, but the night was dark. In the glimmering light from the fire he could see people running to and fro shouting. Many of them he could recognize. They looked so strange in the light of the fire. In some cases he could see only that side of their faces that was illuminated by the blaze. Others seemed to have gaping holes instead of eyes.

It looked as though they were standing out there freezing. That at least wasn't happening to him. He was more than warm enough. The flames came nearer and nearer; if he was going to be rescued it would have to happen fairly soon.

Now he could see his parents out there, too. His mother was dressed in clothes he had never seen before, and his brothers and sisters had cloaks and curtains thrown over their nightdresses. Father was there also, apparently panting after some great strain. He regards with satisfaction the flock of children standing round him. But suddenly he seems to remember something. He looks round his flock once again and then runs back into the burning house. Jackie sees his mother wringing her hands. Can she be cold? Is she sad?

People begin to look up at the window where he is standing. And he hears through the uproar people shouting for someone to fetch a ladder. Others say no, it is too late to go for any ladder, some other method will have to be found that won't take so long.

Then a great strapping fellow runs forward and asks a smaller man to get on his shoulders and the two of them place themselves against the wall. The man on top can now reach as high as the window where John is standing and stretches out his hands to get hold of him. But his foothold slips and down he tumbles. The crowd yells to him that he had better hurry up, and a moment later he is up again. In breathless silence the crowd watches. This time his feet keep steady and John feels himself lifted high up towards the sky by a pair of strong arms, and amid rejoicing and handclapping he is set down upon the ground.

A moment later his father reappears. He had tried in vain to enter the house. Time and time again he had tried to force his way through the flames, but it was impossible. In the end he could do no more than kneel down and commend his son's soul to God. True he had not always been particularly fond of this little boy, for he was a bit too intelligent for Samuel's taste. Indeed, once, half jokingly and half in irritation, he had said to his wife: 'I profess, sweetheart, I think our Jack would not attend to the most pressing necessities of nature unless he could give a reason for it.' But now that the boy was likely to be taken from him, he was truly distracted.

Then he came out and caught sight of John standing there in the cold February night, small and delicate, quiet and unmoved as always. This is too much for Samuel. In wild delight he bursts out: 'Come, neighbours, let us kneel down; let us give thanks to God; He has given me all my eight children; let the house go; I am rich enough.'

There the Wesley family knelt down in the garden of the old rectory and thanked God for saving John from the fire while the remains of the house were collapsing in ashes around them. Little John himself understood but little of what was going on.

Later he learnt that it was Hetty who had noticed the fire first. She had felt something hot fall on her feet, and when she woke saw the ceiling in flames. She shouted 'Fire!', and a few late strollers followed her example. The Rector was roused and at once grasped the seriousness of the situation. He had his wife down in a trice, but just as they reached the heavy front door and were about to open it, the rector remembered he had left his keys upstairs. He was forced to run back up the staircase now already ablaze.

The maid, who had grabbed the baby, Charles, disappeared out of the back door. Some of the daughters tried to get out of the windows, but Susanna, who was expecting a child in less than a month, was in no condition to do the same. When after a while her husband re-appeared with the keys, the fire had got such a hold that only with difficulty and at the third attempt were they able to get through the burning door and out into the open. The fire set light to Susanna's clothes and consumed them.

In all this haste and horror John had been forgotten. His mother saw in his miraculous rescue a sign from God that he was destined for some great rôle in life. When she saw him being lifted out of the burning house, she said with pride and emotion in her voice: 'Is this not a brand plucked out of the burning?'

The Rector had said in his moment of greatness that he was rich enough and did not care about the loss of the house. The fact was, however, that he was now poorer than ever, robbed at one blow of house, furniture, books and inheritance. But as he himself said: 'The world I can always fight, but Providence never.'

Of the old rectory nothing was left. A few bits of old iron and the remains of household utensils were all they found in the ruins. Except, that is, for one thing more: a charred leaf of a Bible that he had greatly prized. It was a valuable Bible, written in several languages, with the texts placed side by side for easy comparison.

Should he view ironically this text that shone out at him from the scorched page, or should he take it as a greeting and encouragement from Him who reigns on high and whose ways seemed to Samuel Wesley to be more than marvellous? For there it stood, in Latin: 'Go and sell all that thou hast and take up your cross and follow me.'

To sell what he had could now be quickly done. And Samuel was now more than ever willing to take up the Cross and follow in the steps of his incomprehensible Master.

The Wesley family was now scattered through the village. John was lodged with a parson and the others found shelter where they could. The strict discipline that Susanna's supervision had ensured was now replaced by something much freer, and the children were in a position to run out and play with the other children as they wished. It was a source of great grief to her, for the children stopped speaking in an educated manner and acquired 'a clownish accent and many rude ways'. They also got to hear about things that they had never had any inkling of before and learned to sing secular songs.

She looked forward, therefore, with great longing to the day when they would be able to move into the new rectory. It was larger and more modern than the old one, but it didn't materialize like a phoenix from the ashes. It took time and cost money. Not until a number of years had elapsed was it completely in order and could be called ready.

When the family was again finally assembled under one roof Susanna energetically set about taking up the threads of what had been neglected. God had placed such a great responsibility upon her. Her daughters were growing older. Their problems must be attended to, and John, too, in particular, needed her. It seemed God surely intended to do something with him.

It was at this time that she began to hold weekly talks with each one of her children individually. It was the turn of the two eldest daughters, Emilia and Sukey, on Sunday, and the other children were each allowed one of the week-days. John's evening was Thursday, and these talks with his mother were to remain with him for the rest of his life.

The attitude of the villagers towards the Wesley family now underwent a marked change. There could be no doubt that it was the Rector's enemies who had started the fire and almost killed a number of innocent people. This caused revulsion in even the most brutish of them, and the way the parson had accepted his loss had aroused the greatest respect among his parishioners. In the end they began to feel proud of this clergyman who like a cleansing storm of the Lord went about the village and chastised them for their sins and participated in their joys and sorrows. The local patriots boasted that no one had such a devil of a rector as they. He was the sort of parson one could be proud of. As a result he was several times chosen to represent the diocese at the Convocation of the Church, meeting in London.

Once again Samuel Wesley travelled to London, but this time it was his good heart and impulsive nature that drove him to it. A minister he knew, a certain Sacheverell, had been charged with preaching doctrines calculated to mislead his congregation. Wesley hurried to London to help in his defence, and he even wrote the defence for the counsel to use. But all this took time, and meanwhile he had installed a locum in his church, while his wife, Susanna, conducted the services at home.

Susanna was sitting reading a book Emilia had brought home with her. She could not remember ever having read any book that interested her so much. Indeed, she became quite heated by her reading, and her eyes shone and her cheeks glowed. The book concerned two Danish missionaries who in a miraculous way had been the instruments of God's work out in the mission field. And surely what could happen out there in heathen parts could also happen here in England? For wasn't God the same everywhere?

While Samuel was in London they had a locum whose only gospel seemed to be that a man must pay his debts. Whatever text he was asked to preach on, he always returned to the same theme. Now

Susanna also heartily agreed that a person ought to pay his debts, but nevertheless, the idea could become somewhat monotonous spiritual food in the long run, and apart from this there was no afternoon service on Sundays while her husband was away.

So Susanna herself assembled her children for their Sunday afternoon devotions. Several of the neighbours heard about this and asked for permission to join. For the first few Sundays there were about forty people present, but gradually more and more came until several hundred were gathered in all the rooms of the rectory and even in the garden outside.

They would begin with a psalm and then Susanna would read one of the best sermons they had in the house. Then they sang another psalm and went straight home. That was all.

John and Charles were also present at these meetings and saw something of the use God could make of women in his Kingdom. This was to prove of use to them when later as grown men they emerged as the leaders and shepherds of the great religious revival.

But there were some who didn't like these meetings. First and foremost there was the locum. He could only manage to collect a handful of people to listen to his observations about the necessity of paying one's debts. And Samuel Wesley, himself, didn't like them either.

He wrote to ask what was it all about, and wondered whether she could not at least get a man to read the sermons?

'Ah,' replied his wife, and there was triumph in her tone, 'you don't know what sort of men these men are. Most of them can't even read, and those who can have to stop at this or that word and spell it out before pronouncing it. And their voices, too, are so weak that they wouldn't carry to all who were present.'

Susanna was of the opinion that it was God who had willed that she should do this thing, but on the other hand she also wanted to bow to the will of her husband and close the meetings if that was really what he wanted. But in that case he must give her an unambiguous order about the matter so that her conscience would be clear and the responsibility his alone.

But no such order came. Instead the Rector himself arrived, a little downcast because the court case had gone badly despite the brilliant oration he had delivered in the defence, and a little peevish because his wife had been more successful in the work of the parish than he had himself.

The locum had not had a very good time. Wesley wished to test him and asked: 'I suppose you can prepare a sermon upon any text I give you?'

'Yes, sir,' answered the locum.

'Then prepare a sermon on Hebrews 11[6]: "Without faith it is impossible to please God".'

'Very good.'

But when the time came for the locum to deliver his sermon and the text had been read, he began thus: 'Friends, faith is a most excellent virtue, and it produces other virtues also. In particular, it makes a man pay his debts.'

Soon afterwards Samuel Wesley, too, was gripped by the family's missionary zeal. He wrote off to the East India Company and offered his services as missionary in some district where the Christian gospel had never yet been proclaimed, if only the company would look after the matter of his stipend and provide a pension in the event of his decease during his missionary activity. But no such support was forthcoming. So he carried on with his work in his own parish—and and occupied himself with Job, the man of affliction. . . .

When John was nearly eleven years old he was sent off to the Charterhouse School in London. The Duke of Buckingham had provided a scholarship for the purpose. The school was really an old monastery that had been vacated and turned into a school. Like the majority of English boys, John remained devoted to his old school the whole of his life, and he is regarded as one of its outstanding pupils, not only because of his later fame but also in the matter of the subjects he studied and his examination results.

Everyone who has read descriptions of the boarding-schools of the day, knows that life for the youngest boys was not exactly a game. John had learnt already at home to accept the food that was placed before him and he was used to managing on very plain fare. Furthermore, he had learnt to 'cry softly'. All this was now to prove unusually helpful to him. One thing he did have to get used to was the fact that the bigger boys took all the meat, and the smaller ones had to be satisfied with bread.

John was never a sportsman. He never had the time to devote to it. But he did find time even at school to keep his body in good condition, and it was here that he laid the foundation of that iron health which later was to be put to such severe test. He rose early in the morning and ran three times round the courtyard, a tiny little fellow in a great big courtyard. Later in life the little man was to face heavy tasks when he rode through the land as a messenger of the Lord. There is something in the saying that the child is father of the man. There is no doubt that some of the characteristics of the future evangelist had their roots in his schooldays at Charterhouse.

Here, too, John Wesley's ability to lead first came to light. He gathered his fellow-pupils about him and told them stories and carried them along by the power of his narrative.

The letters from home were always full of admonitions that he undoubtedly read and followed most exactly. They were always accompanied by exhortations to lead a good life. When later in life he looked back upon this period, he said that in some ways he regarded himself as a Christian even then. In the first place he didn't think his habits were quite so bad as those of others, and he also still had a little attachment left for Christianity. Last of all, he went regularly to church and communion, something he had promised to do as early as his eighth year.

But the letters from home also contained many other things that John read with just as much interest. There was, for instance, the story of the very last inhabitant of the rectory, 'Old Jeffrey', which he read with round-eyed amazement.

Let us, therefore, look in at the rectory at Epworth one winter evening about 1716, while John is away at Charterhouse in London.

The children are lying shuddering with fear. They press close together to protect one another from something dangerous. They are drenched with sweat and stiff with horror.

There it is again!—The wind howls through the trees in the garden and clutches at the ridge of the roof, and now and again an owl sends forth its weird cry into the night. But it is not this that makes the children whine with fear.

Now it is walking slowly up the stairs! White in the face they stare out into the night. So far they have never actually seen anything, only heard. Just imagine if it should enter their room!

They shout to Mother to see if she is awake. How could a person be anything else but awake in this uproar? Susanna finds it difficult to understand how God can permit such a thing as this, and is at a loss to know the meaning of it all. Is it, perhaps, a warning to them, a message from the other world? But in that case, from Heaven or from Hell?

The shuffling has stopped, but now the knocking begins, in the walls and the ceiling. What on earth can it all be?

When this banging first began Susanna had for a long time been anxious lest something should have happened to her son Samuel who was at school in London. During long wakeful nights she had imagined she saw him lying bleeding under horses' hooves or pale and lifeless in a white bed with a candle burning at the head. Because of him she had gone through all the qualms of agony and death. She had written and begged him to answer by return and tell how he was. A short while afterwards they received a letter. All was well with Samuel, it was just that he had had so much to do that for a while he had not found time to write.

When the knocking started, they thought at first that someone was playing a joke on them. Perhaps something of the old enmity was beginning to flare up again? Or was it one of the servants? Perhaps, finally, it was one of their daughters who had hidden one or other of her admirers here during the evening and now he was trying to attract attention in this way.

All possible solutions were discussed and tested. Samuel pursued the phantom from room to room and commanded it in the name of Jesus to reveal itself. But the only answer he got was renewed knocking. And sometimes the ghost was so cheeky that it slammed the door in his face and blew out his candle over and over again.

All doors were opened, all cupboards and drawers examined, all corners combed, but still no trace of the disturber of the peace could be found.

Finally they came to the conclusion that it must be 'Old Jeffrey', who, having failed to find peace in his grave, was now going round rustling and pattering through the night. And thus it was that the ghost came to be known among them as 'Old Jeffrey'.

That 'Old Jeffrey' was a member of the old school with most decided sympathies and antipathies there could be no doubt. He also had very fixed and dogmatic views on politics. He belonged to the Right and was a follower of the Stuart party. When Master Samuel prayed for William of Orange at evening prayers, 'Old Jeffrey' behaved like one possessed and wouldn't leave his political opponent in peace even when he was at work. When, therefore, Susanna, who shared the same political opinions as 'Old Jeffrey', withdrew to her room between five and six o'clock in the afternoon in order to have her regular hour of prayer, the ghost remained as silent as a grave. Never once did he disturb her devotions and contemplation. Thus 'Old Jeffrey' showed himself to be a true cavalier. But even so, he still remained quite inexplicable.

Nor was the knocking ghost any more harmful to the children. The youngest child Kezzy used him as a sort of playmate. When 'Old Jeffrey' knocked she would knock back, just as though she had never done anything else in all her five years of life except speak the ghost's own special language.

The second youngest daughter, Martha, used to hear the ghost pursuing her when she was sweeping the floor. It made almost the same sound as a person using a broom, and she was annoyed that 'Old Jeffrey' should walk after her instead of in front, for then he could have done the work for her. Indeed, the children became so accustomed to the tapping at the bedheads that they would say: '"Old Jeffrey" is coming; now it is time to go to sleep.'

But even though the children succeeded in getting on friendly terms with the ghost, it was still an uncomfortable thing to have about the house. Susanna was naturally grateful for the help she got in her domestic political battle and she also relied upon his chivalry towards her as a woman, but even so she, too, would willingly have been rid of this new member of the family. So she sent a message to a friend of hers, a parson who was reputed far and wide to be a crack hand at driving out evil spirits and ghosts from haunted houses. The man came: he assumed an omniscient air and characterized the occurrence as most interesting—and very dangerous! The flock of children followed him with open mouths as though moved by excitement and they rejoiced when the expert pronounced his finding. But we can well imagine that it was one of the Rector's half-grown daughters, or perhaps even one of the servants, who most enjoyed the expert and all he represented. Perhaps she had thought that in this strictly regulated rectory it would be amusing to try to provide some amusement herself.

No one knows to this day who played the part of the knocking ghost in the rectory at Epworth. We do know, however, that John, who at that time was at boarding-school, read about it in letters from home. That he should believe in ghosts is not really surprising. The greatest literary figure of the age, Dr Samuel Johnson, also believed in ghosts. The unilluminated streets and the houses with their flickering candles would appear to have stimulated such beliefs.

The knocking ghost affected them all in such a way as to strengthen their belief in the hereafter and in the world of evil spirits.

The last glimpse we get of John Wesley as a child is when he, at the age of rather more than sixteen, deemed himself finished with Charterhouse and ready for university. But if he was to go to Oxford, then financial arrangements would have to be made. This had always been the great bugbear.

His father sent him to the minister Sacheverell, whom he had once defended so energetically when he had been accused of preaching pernicious doctrines. So we find the young, dark-haired boy in the presence of this powerful and influential man, with a letter of recommendation from his father in his hand.

Many years later he describes the episode thus:

'I found him alone, as tall as a may-pole, and as fine as an archbishop. I was a very little fellow. . . . He said: "You are too young to go to the University; you cannot know Greek and Latin yet. Go back to school." I looked at him as David looked at Goliath, and despised him in my heart. I thought: "If I do not know Greek and Latin better than you, I ought to go back to school indeed." I left him, and neither entreaties nor commands could have again brought me back to him.'

Here speaks the real John Wesley, the proud and independent son of Susanna. When we think of his work henceforth in life, the simile of David and Goliath does not, perhaps, seem inappropriate.

Chapter IV

In the April of Youth

AT THE early age of ten John had said farewell to his home at Epworth in order to go to school. The next seven years of his life he passed at the Charterhouse, which he left with a scholarship of £40 per annum that enabled him to go to Oxford. Here he arrived on Midsummer Day in the year 1720 just one week after his seventeenth birthday, and he matriculated at Christ Church. In the fifteen years that were to follow he became an integral part of the academic life of Oxford, with but one short break.

What impression the venerable old town with its characteristic towers and spires made on him, we do not know. In his journals he avoids all that could be called descriptive of nature in favour of the attempt to record moods. When it is a question of literature, John can with justice be called a lover of beauty, but there is nothing anywhere to indicate that he could fall into a reverie over a beautiful landscape. The important thing for him was that things around him should be clear and orderly.

Still, it must have been in a glad spirit that he took up his studies as one of the fourth generation of Wesleys at Oxford. His brother Samuel had also been there earlier, but he had now completed his course and was working as a teacher in London.

The university was well provided with books and equipment for study and had large reading-rooms and an extensive library. There was also a series of scholarships available to the students, and he who was so inclined could get as good an education at Oxford as it was possible to procure at the time. But it depended in great measure upon the intentions of the student himself. For never have the standards of this old university been lower than they were in the eighteenth century. The historian Gibbon, who later achieved world fame with his mighty work on the Roman Empire, says that he owed Oxford absolutely nothing.

The tutors collected their payment very punctually, but as a rule this was all the punctuality they practised. The students passed their examinations merely by being in residence for a stipulated period, irrespective of how they worked. Consequently, Oxford became known as a hothouse of vice and immorality, and many acquired there habits of laziness that later they found difficult or impossible to discard.

Established as a condition of entry into the university was the requirement that the student should conform to the doctrine and creed of the Anglican Church, the so-called Thirty-Nine Articles. To these the student had to append his signature, but only a very few ever felt the inclination to read this document through. Religious questions were ridiculed and when it came to practising Christianity, neither teachers nor pupils ever attended more than the three communions required by the regulations.

John Wesley took up his studies with great diligence and interest, without permitting himself to be infected by the spirit and tone of the University. This does not mean that he was any shining example or saint standing apart from all that young men generally regard as amusing. A fellow-student has supplied us with one of the few sketches we have of him from outsiders at this time. He says Wesley was a very sensible young university student with most liberal and manly emotions. He had a reputation for wit and surprised everyone with his subtle and wily logic. If he could inveigle people into a harmless debate and tie them up in knots, he would laugh happily. He took an intellectual pleasure in putting people in the wrong by asking them artful questions—as many young students do.

We really know little about the life he led during these first years of study, but we do get an occasional glimpse of it in the letters he wrote to his parents and brothers and sisters.

Brother Samuel wrote, for instance, asking him to let him see one of his poems. This brother was a bit of a poet himself and was interested in having John follow in his footsteps. In answer to this request, John sent him some poems. The first recorded poem we have of John Wesley is about—a flea! It is the goddess Chloe who is the proud possessor of this little domestic animal. Just as Juno had her favourite parrot and Venus a dove, so Chloe had a flea. This, then, was the type of fun in which John Wesley indulged as a student.

But he also wrote more serious poems. He sent a paraphrase of the 65th Psalm to his father who was enthusiastic about it and expressed the wish that he should not bury his talent. His mother on the other hand said it was all very well to write poems, but 'Make poetry sometimes your diversion, though never your business'.

John Wesley continued writing poems and hymns with ready ease throughout the whole of his life, and on occasion he could rise to great heights. But poetic talent of the kind that his brother Charles possessed was never his.

The letters he exchanged with his father mostly treat of theological matters. He discussed the same type of problem with his mother as long as she lived, but in the correspondence with his father we also see the young John Wesley against the background of everyday life. He told of a smallpox epidemic raging at the college, claiming some victims before being checked. Here, too, were records of strange and fantastic stories he had heard. He mentioned a house in the neighbourhood which was certainly haunted. No one would dare live there, but he had the idea of passing a night there just to see if what they said was true.

It appeared, too, that it was unsafe for young gentlemen to go out at night because of a more palpable kind of enemy. Robbers had made it a sort of trade to steal young men's wigs, and a wig was no trifling expense. So clever had these robbers become that even if the young gentlemen were sitting in a carriage with a hood, they were still prepared to cut a hole in the hood and snatch their perukes away. Not that this played any great part in John Wesley's life personally, for he had no wig. He had allowed his hair to grow long, convinced that this was the healthiest plan. Considering that it was so exceedingly healthy to have long hair, it would never occur to him to squander several pounds per annum on a barber, especially now when his means were so scanty that only with extreme economy could he manage to keep out of debt.

His health was not uniformly good. One day when he was out walking his nose began to bleed. He tried first one thing and then another to stop the bleeding, but without success. The bleeding only stopped when he finally undressed and plunged into the waters of the Thames. These are the sort of isolated glimpses of his life and thought that his letters contain.

And was the young man a true Christian?

He continually received letters from his mother exhorting him to go the way of righteousness. 'Now, in good earnest, resolve to make religion the business of your life; for, after all, that is the one thing that strictly speaking is necessary and all things else were comparatively little to the purposes of life. I heartily wish you would now enter upon a serious examination of yourself, that you may know whether you have a reasonable hope of salvation.'

One conversation he had with one of the servants at the university convinced him that there was something in religion that he had not grasped. This was revealed by the janitor who possessed but one coat and had not had anything to eat that day. Even though he had tasted nothing but water, he was still full of thanks to God.

'You thank God when you have nothing to wear, nothing to eat, and no bed to lie upon. What else do you thank Him for?'

'I thank Him', answered the servant, 'that He has given me life and being; and a heart to love Him, and a desire to serve Him.'

When Wesley himself looked back on these first years at university, he said that he still prayed to God both publicly and privately and that apart from the Scriptures he also read many other religious books, particularly commentaries on the New Testament. 'Yet I had not all this while so much as a notion of inward holiness; nay, went on habitually, and for the most part very contentedly, in some or other known sin: indeed, with some intermission and short struggles, especially before and after the Holy Communion, which I was obliged to receive thrice a year. I cannot well tell what I hoped to be saved by now, when I was continually sinning against that little light I had; unless by those transient fits of what many divines taught me to call repentance.'

But now he was about to experience something which profoundly affected his life and changed a great many things.

Not very far from Oxford lies the little village of Stanton. It was here John Wesley experienced the first tempestuous April of his life.

One of Wesley's friends at the university was a certain Robert Kirkham. He was the son of a clergyman in Stanton and had three sisters whom he was most desirous of presenting to John Wesley. Indeed, he so looked up to Wesley that he rejoiced at the thought of the day when he would be able to consider himself related to him by family ties.

In the rectory at Stanton Wesley passed many happy and carefree hours, a pleasant change from his monastic existence in his little study-cell at Oxford. Here was to be found all that John had had to miss in his youth, all that held attraction for a young man. Here were comfortable and spacious living conditions, with good food and choice wine. The family had strong cultural interests, and for the most part the conversation turned on religion, with literature and music also playing a part. The whole offered a sharp contrast to his own penniless home with its strict puritanical régime.

There were, then, three daughters in the house. To one of them Wesley felt himself strongly attracted. Which one it was, we do not know, for in accordance with the custom of the age the correspondents never used their correct names but gave one another flowery, poetic titles. The young girl elected to be called 'Varanese', and under this name she has been recorded in Wesley's secret diary. It is from here that we draw our knowledge of this rector's daughter in Stanton; probably it was the elder daughter, Sally, who had won Wesley's heart.

This Sally was an enchanting beauty, vivacious and charming. She was also a serious Christian and kept up her reading of devotional works. Wesley says he had the greatest confidence in her wholesome judgement. Varanese filled his bachelor existence with rosy dreams.

The final consequence was that he, who had hitherto been completely convinced that it was best for a man to remain single, now began to give this notion a thorough revision. This young twenty-two-year-old student was now prepared to break with one of his religious principles and get married. But not immediately. He had not the means. In seven years, perhaps; presumably Varanese would wait this long? In any event, he decided not to reveal himself to her. He would visit her home and discuss theology with her and detach himself from university life. But apart from this he would keep his feelings a secret for the next seven years.

It is noteworthy that in this matter he consulted not his mother, but his elder sister Emilia. To her he wrote about his plans—about the golden dream he hoped to realize seven years later.

Emilia was certainly exactly the right person to turn to in an affair of this sort. She was the eldest of the sisters and had had to bear the heaviest burden at home, had twice been deeply in love herself, and had twice seen her family step in and foil her marriage plans. On the first occasion it was her mother and her eldest brother who had not liked her elected and had broken off the connexion, and on the second occasion it was John himself who had strongly cautioned his elder sister against marrying the Quaker doctor with whom she had started a love-affair! Emilia had bowed before what she deemed was God's will. 'My Creator seems to have decreed me to a state of suffering here, and always deprives me of what I love, or embitters it to me. Who can contend with Omnipotence?'

To this bitter and disappointed sister, then, John wrote and unburdened his heart. He must have mentioned something about the seven years he had thought of devoting to the service of his sweetheart, for Emilia wrote back immediately in discouraging strain.

'Whether you will be engaged before thirty or not I cannot determine; but if my advice be worth listening to, never engage your affections before your worldly affairs are in such a posture that you may marry very soon. The contrary practice has proved very pernicious to our family; and were I to live my time over again, and had the same experience I have now, were it for the best man in England, I would not wait one year.'

This letter was dated 7th April 1725. The 10th April saw John travelling post-haste to Stanton. He had a thoughtful expression on his face as he spurred on his horse to arrive in time! Could it be possible that women were unwilling to wait seven years as Rachel and Leah had done? Ten whole days he remained at the rectory, with his soul alternating between hope and fear, 'towering exultation, deadly despair'. They discussed Thomas à Kempis's *Imitation of Christ* and matters of religion while Wesley was longing merely for the intimate conversation he must have with Varanese. Then finally, on 20th April, this conversation took place. He collected his thoughts in his diary, and, as though uttering a prayer, wrote: 'Let it not be in vain!'

But it was in vain! Varanese was to give ear to another, and a young clergyman Jack Chapone was the happy man! Nothing came of Wesley's plans. The dream vanished, the castles in the air crumbled into ruins. The day was no longer so radiant nor life so fair.

A despondent young man now rode back to Oxford after the first major disappointment of his life. The whole of his life he was to long for love, for human affection and his own home, but never was he destined to achieve it. Yet the outcome of this youthful infatuation was to be of importance to the young evangelist who continued to develop and mature as a result of the reverses he experienced, the privations and the self-denials.

Pale and disconsolate he took out his little diary and began to question himself. 'Have I loved woman or company more than God?' he inquired. 'Has this been one of Satan's snares?'

This friendship had influenced Wesley deeply; later he wrote thus about this period of his life: 'Meeting with a religious friend, which I never till now had, I began to alter the whole form of my conversation.' In his journal which he intended for publication, he called Varanese 'a religious friend'. Probably nothing more was ever intended on her side, but meeting her was, nevertheless, sufficient to cause Wesley to change the whole tone of his conversation. Gone was the desire to run around tying people in knots with logical sophistry. Now he starts to be serious.

There is also another reason why the friendship with Varanese was so important for Wesley. With her delight in discovery this young lady had unearthed the old book *Imitation of Christ*. Now Wesley had probably often both seen and heard of this book, but so far he had never read it. During the visit to Stanton he was able to borrow Varanese's copy, and this was the introduction to a work which was destined to influence him profoundly. With Varanese behind him, he was willing to read the book even though the translation was a poor one, and even though he had absolutely no desire to read the original in Latin. The book was not congenial to him. He thought it was too strict. Where was all the happiness of religion? Had not Solomon once said that the paths of religion were full of pleasantness? Where was this delight in Thomas à Kempis? Then, too, he reacted strongly to the doctrine of choice between salvation and perdition, of which he found traces in the book, even though the mode of its expression was considerably smoothed down in the English translation. He discussed the matter with his mother in a letter, and she wrote a long letter to him giving him a whole series of reasons for rejecting the doctrine of choice. Indeed, she actually provided John with the arguments that many years later he was able to use in a great sermon on free grace delivered in opposition to the Calvinist preacher, George Whitefield.

In the same year, in 1725, he had occasion to read another book. This was Bishop Jeremy Taylor's *Rules for Holy Living and Holy Dying*. This latter book was to have absolute and decisive importance for the whole of his life and development.

Chapter V

Turning Point

THE YEAR 1725 proved to be a turning-point in Wesley's religious development. The *Imitation of Christ*, as has been said, influenced him deeply. But the other books, Bishop Jeremy Taylor's *Rule and Exercises of a Holy Living* and *Rule and Exercises of Holy Dying*, were to have a more direct effect.

It was particularly Taylor's fundamental demand for purity of intention that roused John Wesley. He saw now that he must begin to investigate the whole of his life, not merely its outward manifestations but also the motives and reasons that prompted them. Taylor had awakened in him a longing for a personal piety.

Now it was a question of finding a way of controlling himself, and the idea for this, too, he found in Taylor. Thus the latter can be regarded as one of the formative influences of Methodism, at least in the form it assumed at the University of Oxford. Prompted by Taylor, Wesley began to keep a diary in which all his thoughts and feelings were accurately noted down.

He kept two types of diary. One was copious and detailed and intended for publication. Wesley himself issued it later in summary form. This is the diary we call the *Journal* and it can safely be regarded as one of the major works of the period. Here we read about the people with whom Wesley came into contact, about the conversations he had with them and the impression they made on him. Here, too, are the stories he heard and not least, of course, the record of the gatherings in which he took part, of the conflicts he had with the rabble, the clergy, and the Church. We see what books he read and how they impressed him. Wesley's *Journal* is a good portrait of his age, of people and conditions of life as they were then, an important primary source both for the study of John Wesley's own character and of the movement he instigated in England and caused to spread throughout the world.

But the record he now began to keep, the 'Diary', was of a totally different nature. It was not intended for publication, but was, on the contrary, intended as a secret reflection of himself. He kept it locked away and for further protection against the possibility of others reading what he had written, he employed symbols, codes, shorthand, abbreviations, and pseudonyms.

For a long time, it remained impossible for anyone to read the diary, but finally a Methodist minister named Nehemiah Curnock succeeded, after a prodigious labour of patience, in penetrating Wesley's inner and secret world. What were the intimate secrets Wesley had been brooding over since he had taken such pains to cover his tracks? With curiosity and expectation both friends and opponents assailed the confidences the great evangelist had recorded many years before.

Those who had expected to find something which would reduce the stature of the man Wesley were disappointed. Time and time again he had been blamed for hideous sins as he stood in the midst of the movement that God had raised up through him. He found himself obliged to issue disavowals and assurances of his innocence. Would the diary reveal interesting facts about such things as this?

There is no doubt that the diary gives us a more human and intimate view of Wesley than his other works. But we find his charge-sheet clean. Crystal-clear and pure was his character, even if we often find him writhing under temptation and discovering sin where a less scrupulous person would have seen nothing wrong. Mercilessly he exposes to the light his inclination towards what is evil, without trying to excuse himself or explain the matter away.

The book begins thus:

'*A General Rule in All Actions of Life*

Whenever you are to do an action, consider how God did or would do the like, and do you imitate His example.

General Rules of Employing Time

1. Begin and end every day with God; and sleep not immoderately.
2. Be diligent in your calling.
3. Employ all spare hours in religion; as able;
4. All holidays [i.e. holy-days].
5. Avoid drunkards and busybodies.
6. Avoid curiosity, and all useless employments and knowledge.
7. Examine yourself every night.
8. Never on any account pass a day without setting aside at least an hour for devotion.
9. Avoid all manner of passion.'

Then a little extract for Friday, 26th March 1725:

'I found a great many unclean thoughts arise in prayer, and discovered these temptations to it:

(a) Too much addicting myself to a light behaviour at all times.
(b) Listening too much to idle talk, or reading vain plays or books.
(c) Idleness, and lastly

Want of devotion—consideration in whose presence I am.
From which I perceive it is necessary

(a) To labour for a grave and modest carriage;
(b) To avoid vain and light company; and
(c) To entertain awful apprehensions of the presence of God.
(d) To avoid idleness, freedom with women, and high-seasoned meats;
(e) To resist the very beginnings of lust, not by arguing with, but by thinking no more of it or by immediately going into company; lastly
To use frequent and fervent Prayer.

General Rules as to Intention

1. In every action reflect on your end;
2. Begin every action in the name of the Father, the Son, and the Holy Ghost;
3. Begin every important work with prayer;
4. Do not leave off a duty because you are tempted in it.'

These are some of the general rules by which Wesley was now to begin to live. It is a serious striving for holiness and purity right down to the innermost depths of his soul that is here revealed. He had already realized earlier that religion resides in the heart. Now he accepts the consequences and begins with great power and energy and with the help of the best methods the difficult task of purifying his heart.

Wesley saw that one of the most important things in attaining sanctification was the correct use of one's time. Time was the most precious and most irretrievable of all God's gifts. Therefore it had to be used properly. He discovered that he often lay awake for an hour or more during the night, so he concluded that he was taking more sleep than his system required. Next morning he rose early, at six o'clock. But the next night also he lay awake for a whole hour. Consequently, the following evening he set the alarm clock to ring at five o'clock and rose then. Even so he didn't succeed in sleeping the whole of the next night through, but woke up and lay tossing and turning for the space of an hour after midnight. The next morning the alarm clock was set for four o'clock, and there it remained for the rest of his life.

'Leisure and I have taken leave of one another,' he wrote to his brother Samuel. Never again were they to meet.

It was also about this time that the future winner of souls found his first soul. He and a friend were at a funeral at St Mary's Church, and on the way home Wesley led the conversation along serious channels. Suddenly breaking off, he asked his friend if he really was his friend.

'Yes, indeed,' was the reply. 'Then you will not refuse to do your friend a service?' 'Of course not!' 'Then my friend must permit me to make him a true and real Christian, for that is my greatest wish!' It appears that the friend was very much affected by Wesley's words, and when a short time later he died of tuberculosis Wesley spoke at his grave as his friend had asked him to do.

It was in the same year, 1725, that Wesley seriously decided to become a minister. He had been thinking about it for a long time, and perhaps the prospect of being able to get married had been not the least part of the attraction. At any rate his father wrote to him saying that he ought not to enter into the service of the Church merely 'to get a piece of bread'. A man ought to be impelled by much higher motives than this before entering the ministry. On the contrary, Wesley ought to dedicate himself to 'critical learning'.

Susanna, on the other hand, was very anxious that John should be ordained and surrender himself more completely to God's service. Soon her husband Samuel's viewpoint changed too, with the result that John, on 19th September 1725, was ordained deacon, that is, the first and lowest ordination in the Anglican Church. Not until three years later did he receive ordination as priest.

It was difficult to find the money that was needed for John's ordination. His father had already managed to work up a new debt. An uncle from India was expected home, and Susanna travelled all the way to London in order to meet him. This uncle was reputed to be so rich that there would be enough to meet both commitments when he arrived. The boat came—but there was no uncle on board. All the same, the ordination fee was raised.

Meanwhile, John continued his studies at the University. A Fellowship became vacant at Lincoln College, Oxford, and John was unanimously elected to the post on 17th March 1726. A Fellow is approximately equivalent to a university scholarship holder or a junior lecturer, and accompanying this position were a regular salary and the right to a room in the college. John continued to receive a salary from his college right up to the day he married many years later. Lincoln College was intended mainly for students from the county of Lincoln. At the time of its foundation, a person was suspect if he held Protestant sympathies. Consequently, it was laid down in the regulations of this institution that it must fight heresy and heretics and those who were elected Fellows had to swear that they would take up this struggle.

The position of Fellow was a position which commanded respect, and in addition it gave a certain economic security. Samuel Wesley talked with pride about his son who was a Fellow at Oxford.

There were other advantages, too. Wesley now enjoyed greater freedom in the choice of subjects he particularly wished to study, and with iron self-discipline he set to work. He had fixed hours for study both in the morning and in the evening, and he permitted nothing to disturb his habits of learning.

On Mondays and Tuesdays, he studied Latin and Greek, on Wednesdays, logic and ethics, on Thursdays, Hebrew and Arabic, on Fridays, metaphysics and natural philosophy, on Saturdays, rhetoric and poetics, and on Sundays, theology. Thus, anyone who possessed a calendar and a clock could say in advance what subject he would be reading at any moment.

In his spare time he read French; later he also taught himself German and Italian well enough to be able to read prayers in these tongues and to be able to converse with Germans and Italians. He translated hymns from all these languages and even one from Spanish, in which exercise he was probably helped by his Latin.

His work at the University consisted now for the most part in the teaching of Greek. Every single week he gave lectures on passages from the Greek New Testament and this forced him to make a thorough study of this field, something which obviously was to be of great use to him later. He was also Moderator, that is, he directed the daily disputations at the University. These were on a very lofty plane, but all the same they were calculated to set the minds of the participators in a turmoil. Here was needed all his sharpness and knowledge of formal logic, and Wesley himself said later that he could not give thanks enough for the practice he got here at discovering the weak points in the apparently crushing arguments of his opponents.

Through the whole of his life, Wesley bore the stamp of his years at the University. He never stooped to cheap effects either in his preaching or in his appearance. Everything was always sparklingly logical and clear, dignified and cultivated. Even so, when later the fire of God caught hold of all the material he had collected it was destined to have an effect on his hearers that even the most popular evangelistic preachers could not attain.

He took his degree of Master of Arts in 1727. His three treatises were particularly well-written and aroused respect in university circles.

Wesley, however, was not tempted by academic honour and renown. He knew that he must enter into solitude with God and his own soul. Intercourse with people was apt to destroy his zeal for holiness. He got to know of a school up in a narrow valley where there was little or no opportunity for enjoying the company of other people. When the teachers there had finished their work for the day they were thrown back entirely upon themselves. Visits from people from other parts of the country hardly ever occurred. Those who told Wesley about this school mentioned it as an example of how cheerless the lot of a teacher can be, cut off like this from all chance of enjoyment and the company of others, but for Wesley it was an enticing description of something that seemed to him almost an earthly paradise. Here he could be quite alone with his studies, no fellow-students or colleagues could come into his room and disturb him. Here, perhaps, he might finally come to live a holy life of strict obedience in accordance with the rules of Bishop Taylor?

Nothing came of it, however, and Wesley did not seek the position. But the strong impression the description of this lonely place made on him shows how compelling was his main aspiration at this time to become a completely pious person.

At home in Epworth Samuel Wesley was still working on his book about Job, but the work was not going quite as smoothly as he wished. He was continually being visited by debt-collectors, for he had managed to work up quite a considerable debt on the book.

Age, too, had begun to claim its right. A stroke had partly paralysed him on one side, making his steps heavy and the stairs long. His eyes saw dimly in the flickering light of the candelabrum. In addition, the amount of his parochial work had increased, for he had secured a small additional living, the parish of Wroot. This added charge brought added difficulties, for during the better part of the year the floods made it difficult to reach, and on two occasions at least the old Rector had been in mortal danger when journeying to or from Wroot.

The matter was clear. Samuel would have to have a curate.

First he wrote to his eldest son, Samuel, and begged him insistently to come and be his curate. Samuel prudently declined. Then the application was addressed to John. It should just suit him now that he was ordained and receiving a salary as a Fellow. It was not very easy to get a curate who was both cheap and also able to put up with an old man.

But John was not inclined to accept, either. He shuddered at the thought of leaving the castle he had built up as a protection against life's many temptations to laziness and intercourse with people who might lead him away from the path of virtue and holiness. With great energy and clear consistency he had transformed life at Oxford into a sort of hothouse for his own personal sanctity, and he shrank from the thought of the violence and crudeness of the lives of profane men.

The matter ended, nevertheless, with John travelling home and taking up a position as curate in his father's parish. Now he was to have under his pastoral care not only his parents whom he is meeting on an equal footing, but also some of his brothers and sisters.

There was scanty light and happiness in the rectory at this time. The shadow of Hetty's downfall hung heavily over the home and left its mark on their conversations. Samuel would have none of Hetty's young man, so she had eloped. But when it came to the point, her lover had shown no sign of wanting to marry her, and crushed and broken she had returned home. Her father was so scandalized that he could not tolerate hearing her name mentioned. Hetty's mother and Emilia were also badly shaken by her behaviour. Samuel forced her to marry forthwith a travelling plumber and glazier named Wright, a none too respectable character, and John must have been saddened by the lot of this elder sister of his who had so often cheered him with her amusing letters and verses.

The time he spent at Wroot John used for further study, the writing of sermons both for himself and for his father, work on the book about Job that he was helping his father with, visiting, and not least the enjoyment of the company of his sisters, some of whom were still at home. He could make life a little easier for them by purchasing those trifles at Wroot market that they had always longed to own but had never been able to acquire because of the strict economies enforced at home.

This remained Wesley's only experience as a parish priest. True, immediately after ordination he had received a sort of curacy in the vicinity of Oxford, but there all he could do was to ride out on Sundays and deliver a sermon. Here in Wroot, on the other hand, he engaged in proper parish work, without, however, being more successful in it than any other average minister of the day.

'From the year 1725 to 1729 I preached much, but saw no fruit of my labour. Indeed it could not be that I should; for I neither laid the foundation of repentance, nor of believing the gospel; taking it for granted, that all to whom I preached were believers, and that many of them "needed no repentance".'

But many years later, when his teaching had become inspired, he wrote in his diary after describing his visits to Epworth and Wroot in 1742: 'Let none think his labour of love is lost because the fruit does not immediately appear! Near forty years did my father labour here, but he saw little fruit of all his labour. I took some pains among this people too, and my strength also seemed spent in vain; but now the fruit appeared. There were scarce any in the town on whom either my father or I had taken any pains formerly; but the seed; sown so long since, now sprung up, bringing forth repentance and remission of sins.'

Nevertheless, he must have felt it as a sort of deliverance when in 1729 he received a letter from the rector at Lincoln College with instructions to return to the University, as it had been decided all Fellows must attend to their duties personally. In a happy frame of mind he travelled back to Oxford, his stronghold, after a term of office as a clergyman, during which time he had distinguished himself in no way at all.

Chapter VI

Oxford Methodist

DURING HIS stay in Wroot, John Wesley had received this good advice from 'a serious man': 'You wish to serve God and go to Heaven. Remember that you cannot serve him alone. You must therefore find companions or make them. The Bible knows nothing of solitary religion.'

These words made a strong impression on Wesley and changed his attitude towards religion. He had been striving in solitude to become a holy man and had devoted all his interest to this struggle, but now it appeared that being holy was a group occupation, something that could not be managed without help from others.

When he now returned to Oxford in 1729 it appeared that there was already a little group there waiting for him to take over the leadership of their work. The group was not large. First and foremost there was his brother, Charles, next a man called William Morgan, and finally Robert Kirkham.

Charles Wesley can be called the founder of Oxford Methodism. He was four years younger than John, being born on 18th December 1707, the eighteenth child. When he was nine years old he entered the well-known Westminster School. The eldest brother, Samuel, who had married the daughter of a parish priest who also ran a boarding-house for boys from Westminster School, had taken charge of Charles from the time that he was little and had been like a father to him. In this way, he had been able to help his hard-pressed father. A little later Charles became a King's scholar, and became Captain of the School in 1725.

In Charles Wesley's youth it is related that he was invited to become the heir of a certain Garrett Wesley, a member of the Irish branch of the family. This Garrett Wesley was immensely rich but had no heirs, and he therefore inquired whether Charles was willing to be his heir. After a long struggle and serious deliberation, Charles refused, and the inheritance went to another branch of the family, to which the famous Arthur Wellesley, Duke of Wellington, later belonged.

Charles had gone to Oxford and matriculated at Christ Church about the same time that John was elected Fellow at Lincoln.

At first he utilized to the full the freedom offered by the University. Not that he indulged in any excesses, but John, in particular, was of the opinion that he did not take his religion seriously enough. 'What! Would you have me be a saint all at once?' was Charles's answer when John rebuked him.

Charles was just as ardent and abrupt in his manner as John was quiet and thoughtful. He used to burst in on his brother in his room in Lincoln College, declaim part of a poem, go over the papers on the desk, look through them with his near-sighted eyes and examine what he wished, and pour out a stream of questions and observations without waiting for a reply from his balanced and methodical brother.

One of his friends at this period who later became leader of the Moravian Brethren in England, John Gambold, describes Charles Wesley thus:

'I never observed any person have a more real deference for another than he had for his brother. . . . Indeed he followed his brother entirely; could I describe one of them I should describe both. I shall therefore say no more of Charles, but that he was a man formed for friendship, who by his cheerfulness and vivacity would refresh his friend's heart with attentive consideration, would enter into, and settle all his concerns as far as he was able.'

While John was in Epworth and Wroot as his father's assistant, Charles was seriously moved by God and started to meditate. He, too, felt the desire to begin leading a holy life. But it was not natural for him to shut himself up in his study and meditate in solitude. He gathered some friends together, and they met regularly each Sunday at first, and later twice a week. Their object was to study the Greek New Testament and otherwise help one another by reading and a serious Christian way of living within the framework of university life.

When John returned from Wroot, it was quite natural that he should slip into this circle, indeed, they immediately chose him as the very man to be their leader. Now he had been given the opportunity of practising religion in the company of others.

They could not complain about lack of attention, this little group of men who were filled with the desire to take Christianity seriously and try to live according to the rules advocated by the University. They were called the 'Godly Club', the 'Reform Club', 'Bible Moths', 'Sacramentarians', 'Enthusiasts', and many more names, but the titles that stuck to the group were the 'Holy Club' and 'Methodists'.

The name 'Methodist' was actually used as a medical term among the Catholics who thought they could cure all sorts of sickness by a special method which consisted essentially of diet and exercise. When now these men in Oxford began to live in their methodical way in order to attain inner holiness, somebody remarked, 'Here is a new set of Methodists sprung up', and so the name stuck to them as a term of abuse. Later they came to adopt it as a title of honour.

It is interesting to see what an opponent of the 'Holy Club' had to say about them. One of the group's most zealous members, William Morgan, had become deranged as a result of the great strain they lived under and died at his home in Ireland in a state of mental disorder. He had a younger brother who was also with the group for a time, but he broke away and later gave this description of the meetings:

'They imagine they cannot be saved if they do not spend every hour, nay every minute, of their lives in the service of God. . . . They almost starve themselves to be able to relieve the poor and buy books for their conversions. They endeavour to reform notorious whores and allay spirits in haunted houses. They fast two days in the week, which has emaciated them to that degree that they they are a frightful sight. . . . They are become the jest of the whole University. . . . They often cry for five minutes for their sins; then lift up their heads and eyes, and return God thanks for the great mercies He has showed them in granting them such repentance, and then laugh immoderately as if they were mad.'

This is how the group appeared to a Philistine. Even if it is depicted in critical and unsympathetic colours, it is still very acutely observed. One sees how seriously these men took their Christianity, how they explored their souls and tried to reach their innermost selves. The young man who gave this description had not been able to endure the powerful spiritual excitements involved, and in the long run John, too, was on the way to destroying himself. He could thank his iron constitution that things went as well as they did.

Every Wednesday and Friday were considered special fast days. What they saved in this way they gave to the poor and needy. John Wesley reduced his personal expenditure to twenty-eight pounds a year. He earned thirty pounds and thus was in a position to give away two. In the following year he earned sixty pounds and so was able to give away thirty-two. In the third year his income was trebled and Wesley could give away sixty-two pounds, and in the fourth year ninety-two. He sold his paintings to help the poor, and denied himself essentials in order to have something to give. He it is who has given posterity the following rule of life: 'Gain all you can! Save all you can! Give all you can!'

Gradually the activities of the 'Holy Club' were developed to include meetings every evening from six o'clock until nine o'clock. They began their meetings with prayers and psalms, and then proceeded with the study of the Greek New Testament. The old classics were also diligently studied and discussed. Wesley's style is witness to his intimate knowledge of these authors. He cites them with ease, and his own style is classically simple and clear.

It was the religious aspect of their work, however, that was paramount for the group, and all other studies were subordinated to this one great aim: to lead a holy life. Every hour of the day they prayed for the fruits of the Holy Spirit, gentleness and humility. Several minutes of every new working hour were devoted to prayer. This might sometimes assume the character of thanks, sometimes of adoration, but most often it was a call to God not to desert them.

They went so methodically to work that they prayed for a special virtue for each day. On one day, for example, their prayer was dedicated to humility. Then they would examine all their thoughts, words, and deeds throughout the day to see if they were humble, and they prayed for more of the same quality if they found out that they needed it, and gave thanks if they thought they had discovered the signs of humility in their lives.

On Sundays they went to communion, not only on the three Sundays prescribed for each year, but every single Sunday. Sunday was dedicated to a scrutiny of the heart and thoughts about God's love and love of one's fellow men. Had they opened their hearts to God's love? Were they living in it every day? Did they love their fellow men? Was their love such that they made a distinction between people, or such that they said to men that they should go in peace and yet failed to give them that which their bodies needed?

Thus they questioned themselves each day and took themselves to task if they found anything that they thought was sinful. They were also obliged to speak out openly to one another if they found anything wrong in one another's lives.

A great change occured one day in 1730 when William Morgan came and announced that he had visited prisoners in jail. He thought they would want to serve his Master and follow his example in this work. Wesley was immediately enthusiastic about the idea, but all the same preferred to write to his father first and ask his advice. He was extremely anxious that these good deeds should not be misunderstood and ridiculed. What did his father think about it?

His father wrote back a fiery letter to say that in the main he approved of their plans. Did anyone believe Satan's servants were dead, in as much as they had reason to expect ridicule? No, Satan's servants were still alive, and they would mock the club's work and make it difficult, but there was no need to take them into their reckonings. On the other hand, they ought first to obtain permission from the person acting as the prison chaplain, so that they would not interfere unlawfully with his work.

Samuel Wesley had himself in his youth at Oxford visited prisoners, and John's grandfather, John Westley, had done the same before him. The idea, therefore, was no new one.

Nevertheless, it was in this way that Methodism's world-wide social work started. For this reason its origins are of peculiar interest.

The Methodists visited the prisoners, freed from debtors' jails those whose debts were not too large for the club to pay off, instructed the prisoners, taught them to read and gave them books on Christianity. In addition they cared for the sick and the needy in the town, and gave free tuition to poor children who otherwise would never have received any education.

'In 1730 I began visiting the prisons; assisting the poor and sick in town; and doing what other good I could, by my presence or my little fortune, to the bodies and souls of all men. To this end I abridged myself of all superfluities, and many that are called necessaries of life. I soon became a by-word for so doing, and I rejoiced that my name was cast out as evil. The next spring I began observing the Wednesday and Friday Fasts, commonly observed in the ancient Church; tasting no food till three in the afternoon. And now I knew not how to go any further. I diligently strove against all sin. I omitted no sort of self-denial which I thought lawful; I carefully used, both in public and in private, all the means of grace at all opportunities. I omitted no occasion of doing good; I for that reason suffered evil. And all this I knew to be nothing, unless as it was directed toward inward holiness.'

This little passage from his diary was written after he had experienced the liberating salvation of belief in Jesus Christ. Then he looked back at the time in Oxford and gives this description of his struggle to become holy. He was nearly dead from starvation and had gone a long way in the matter of mastering his own inclinations. But inner peace he had not attained.

Hence the diary continues thus:

'Accordingly this, the image of God, was what I aimed at in all, by doing His will, not my own. Yet when, after continuing some years in this course, I apprehended myself to be near death, I could not find that all this gave me any comfort or any assurance of acceptance with God. At this I was then not a little surprised; not imagining I had been all this time building on the sand, nor considering that "other foundation can no man lay than that which is laid" by God, "even Christ Jesus".'

During this period the 'Holy Club' got several new members. One of these was Benjamin Ingham, who later accompanied the Wesley brothers to America. And there was John Gambold, who became leader and bishop of the English Synod of the Moravian Church, the Unitas Fratrum of Herrnhut. The most important new member to appear, however, was George Whitefield, later one of England's greatest orators and God-favoured evangelists, leader of the Calvinist branch of Methodism.

When George Whitefield went up to Oxford to study, news about the Wesley brothers and their work had reached his ears and so seized him that he had no higher wish than to obtain permission to become a member. But he found no opportunity of becoming acquainted with the members of the club. Then one day he heard about a woman in one of the poorhouses who had tried to take her life by cutting her throat and sent a message to Charles Wesley about the matter. In this way began a friendship which has carved itself into England's Church history and which had great importance for the religious revival that was to break out later.

At this period John Wesley found another way of putting his time to the most profitable use. On a long walking tour of more than a hundred miles that he undertook with his brother Charles, he discovered that it was possible to read while walking. Later, when he travelled round England on horseback, he read continually, and when he had become so old that he had to drive in a carriage, his books went with him. He also found out that 'the motion and sun together, in our last hundred-and-fifty miles' walk, so throughly carried off all our superfluous humours, that we continue perfectly in health'.

Certain new books fell into Wesley's hands about this time. They were written by one of the period's most important Christian authors, William Law, and had a great influence on Wesley. He also began to read the writings of the old mystics, particularly a work entitled *Theologia Germanica*, but he soon gave up this reading and later said of the mystics that all other enemies of Christendom are trifling compared with them. They are the most dangerous because they hit Christendom in its vital parts.

Samuel Wesley was now beginning to realize that his long struggle against debt-collectors and Dissenters would soon be over. As Charles wrote later to his brother Samuel who was a teacher in Tiverton in the West Country, his father's last thoughts were 'of finishing Job, paying his debts, and seeing you'.

In the meantime, however, Samuel was very anxious to have one of his sons to carry on as Rector of Epworth. First he turned to his eldest son, Samuel, and bade him apply for it, but he refused. Then the request was made to John. But John was not willing to leave Oxford, and in a long letter home he gives no less than twenty-six reasons for remaining in Oxford rather than returning to Epworth. In Oxford he was not disturbed by worldly people or lukewarm Christians; he could be more pious in Oxford and there he was also in a better position to further piety among others.

In a wonderfully sound and rational letter the father waved aside all his son's objections. 'It is not dear self, but the glory of God, and the different degrees of promoting it, which should be our main consideration in the choice of any course of life.'

A few weeks before his father's death, John Wesley tried to secure the parish living, but it was too late. The rectory and the rectory lands which had cost his father so much to acquire, were now to go out of the family to someone whom Samuel regarded with infinite aversion, because, among other things, he was so prodigiously fond of fox-hunting!

On the 25th April 1735, Samuel Wesley died. John was present at his death-bed and read the old prayer expressing the wish that God would accept the dying person into his everlasting abode.

'Now you have done all,' whispered the old man when John had finished the prayer.

To Emilia, his eldest daughter, he said: 'Do not be concerned at my death. God will then begin to manifest himself to my family.'

To John he said: 'The inward witness, son, the inward witness, that is the proof, the strongest proof of Christianity.'

'Sir, are you in much pain?' asked John.

'God does chasten me with pain, yea, all my bones with strong pain; but I thank him for all, I bless Him for all, I love Him for all!'

To Charles: 'Be steady. The Christian faith will surely revive in this kingdom. You shall see it, though I shall not.'

As always, Susanna proved herself splendidly in this hour of trial. Scarcely had Samuel closed his eyes in death before the creditors appeared and laid claim to the whole of the rectory live-stock. Without a farthing she was still able to face the future with trust and confidence. John managed to avert the disaster by paying off his father's debts, but no security for his mother's future could be found.

However, 'Job' was now finished, and with beating heart, John travelled to London to be presented to the Queen and lay this precious family jewel at her feet.

He was received in audience by Queen Caroline, still in her first youth. When John was conducted into the chamber where she was, he found her romping with her ladies-in-waiting. He approached her, bowed on one knee as prescribed by court etiquette and handed her the first copy of the book. She received it coquettishly, turned, examined it, and placed it aside on a shelf without even opening it.

'It is very prettily bound,' she said.

Such was the fate of the book about Job, which for a series of years had been the Wesley family's daily topic of conversation and item of expenditure, and which probably has had very few subsequent readers. All the same, John's journey to London was to be of far-reaching importance to the Wesley family, for it was here he met James Edward Oglethorpe, governor of the colony of Georgia in North America.

Chapter VII

Unsure Ground

JAMES EDWARD OGLETHORPE had a brilliant career behind him and an uncertain future ahead. He was a General and a Member of Parliament and had great influence in leading circles. It was on his initiative that a committee was set up to examine and improve conditions in the prisons. He was ever anxious to come to the aid of those who were really in need.

Oglethorpe had obtained permission from the authorities to establish the colony of Georgia as an asylum for those who had to leave England because their beliefs deviated from the teaching of the Established Church. The land of the redskins was free and offered new opportunities to those whose lives for one reason or another had gone wrong.

Many leading men strongly favoured Oglethorpe's idea. Old Samuel Wesley wrote an enthusiastic letter to him and urged him most strongly to continue, and one of Wesley's friends, Doctor Burton of Oxford, became one of the colony's new representatives or trustees, who, operating from the homeland, were to control the colony's economy and development.

The population of Georgia was fairly heterogeneous. Here were English town-dwellers fleeing from slum conditions. Here were German Moravian Brethren and Scottish highlanders, Italians and Jews. Not a few of the inhabitants were law-breakers fleeing from the arm of the law.

To fuse all these national groups into a single society was no light task, and the fact that the colony lay alongside Spanish territory was not calculated to make the task any easier. It demanded increased watchfulness and created extra difficulties. That Oglethorpe was so successful in spite of this, has gained him a place among England's great empire builders.

There were very few officials willing to give up their secure positions in England in order to travel to the wild and barbaric land several months away by boat.

When Wesley was in London delivering his father's book to Queen Caroline, he was presented to Oglethorpe by Doctor Burton. Burton encouraged the brothers Wesley to go to Georgia and take up missionary work among the Indians there.

As we have heard, missionary work was no new thing in Wesley's family. Both his father and grandfather had occupied themselves with it. His mother had also been deeply moved by the description of the two Danish missionaries and secretly in her heart would gladly have followed their example.

Should John regard this as a call from God? As he had so often done before, he turned to his mother for advice. Susanna was at the time visiting her eldest daughter Emilia, and she replied promptly that 'had I twenty sons, I should rejoice that they were all so employed, though I should never see them more'.

Thus there was no lack of support from home. But was there any other reason for his going? He says himself: 'My chief motive . . . is the hope of saving my own soul. . . . Neither can I hope to attain the same degree of holiness here which I may there.'

To understand this astonishing line of argument, we must first of all remember that Wesley was filled with, almost obsessed by, a single great purpose, to become a man of God. He thought he could best attain this in the company of other pious or uncorrupted people. It was for this reason that he was unwilling to forsake his studies in Oxford and become parish priest in sinful Epworth.

Why, therefore, did Wesley think that he would become holier in the heathen and savage colonial settlement in Georgia?

The dominating thought of the age was 'Back to Nature'. The French thinker Rousseau first coined the catchword. Gradually the idea penetrated the universal mind; many paintings portrayed idyllic pastoral scenes, and poets glorified the simple and uncomplicated life untouched by the corrupting influence of civilization.

In the new colony across the ocean there would surely be ample opportunity of cultivating individual holiness, all the more so because here were to be found real Indians who lived still largely unaffected by the culture of the white man.

There can be no doubt that it was such enthusiastic thoughts that drove the brothers Wesley across the sea. Before John met the Indians he wrote: 'They have no comments to construe away the text; no vain philosophy to corrupt it; no luxurious, sensual, covetous, ambitious expounders to soften its unpleasing truths. . . . They are as little children, humble, willing to learn, and eager to do the will of God.'

In this background it is interesting to read about the same Indians after he has learnt to know them better. They are now 'gluttons, drunkards, thieves, dissemblers, liars . . . ; murderers of fathers, murderers of mothers, murderers of their own children'. It is probable that the actual truth of the matter lies somewhere between these two emotional outbursts of Wesley.

Meantime, however, it was the ideal of personal holiness that drove

Wesley to become a missionary to the Indians. In addition, he consented to act as minister to the white population until somebody else could be procured.

Charles Wesley was given the position of secretary to Oglethorpe —a post for which he was in no way qualified. These vague appointments were to cause the two brothers many difficulties.

Charles had only just been ordained, and he gave his first sermon on the journey over.

With Wesley's departure from London his celebrated *Journal* was begun, which apart from being a remarkable piece of literature is also a primary source of information for everyone who wishes to understand Wesley and his age.

'1735. October 14. *Tues.*—About nine in the morning Mr Benjamin Ingham, of Queen's College, Oxford, Mr Charles Delamotte, son of a sugar merchant, in London, aged twenty-one, who had offered himself some days before, and showed an earnest desire to bear us company, my brother Charles Wesley, and myself, took boat for Gravesend, in order to embark for Georgia.'

The young men who thus set out into the world together were four of the most active Oxford Methodists. 'Our end in leaving our native country was not to avoid want, God having given us plenty of temporal blessings . . . but singly this—to save our souls, to live wholly to the glory of God.'

The four friends had cabins right in the bows of the ship called *Simmonds*. Here they thought they would be least likely to be disturbed. They started straightaway to carry on with the strict over-disciplined life they had led in Oxford. True, they no longer had the books from the University to consult, but they had brought many volumes with them. They rose at four o'clock in the morning and kept things going without a pause until nine or ten o'clock at night.

The very day after they had come on board Wesley began to study German so that he would be able to converse with some Germans who were also on the ship. These were twenty-six 'Herrnhuter' or members of the Brethren of Herrnhut. They had a bishop with them named David Nitschmann.

Apart from the Germans there were also about eighty English emigrants on board the little two-hundred-ton sailing-ship. They were to be accompanied by another British emigrant vessel of the same size and a little warship, the *Hawk*, which was to be used for the defence of the colony. During the storm that later blew up the three ships were separated. The boats were delayed so long by unfavourable weather and storms that they did not leave the harbour at Cowes until the 10th December 1735—nearly two months after the four friends had left London.

Wesley persevered with his pastoral work on board, and when the weather was not too bad, he went from cabin to cabin just as his father had gone from house to house in Epworth. He read and exhorted and prayed. He also baptized a Quaker family who were later numbered among his staunchest friends in America, and he held divine services so often that many of the passengers thought it altogether too much of a good thing. Communion services were held once a week and the number of those who attended was carefully entered in the *Journal*.

The two brothers discussed everything with one another and as a rule they were in agreement. There was, however, a certain Mrs Hawkins, a surgeon's wife who was to be the cause of trouble between them. Ugly rumours about her circulated on board and the others wanted to deny her access to the Lord's Supper. But to Wesley she introduced herself as a repentant sinner and he believed she was sincere. Later this lady was to be the cause of both brothers nearly losing their lives.

Wesley's work with Mrs Hawkins gives evidence of his enormous tolerance and belief in his fellow men which has sometimes been labelled simplicity. Later experiences doubtless made him more sceptical, but it is a fact that he seldom managed to see through a dishonest person, least of all a dishonest woman. The women Wesley had so far enjoyed intimate contact with had all been highly educated —his mother, his sisters, Varanese. On the *Simmonds* he encountered for perhaps the first time active wickedness and duplicity.

But first he had to undergo other shocks. On 25th January 1736 the ship encountered a great storm. True to habit, Wesley examined himself under these new and unusual conditions and found to his horror that he was afraid, mortally afraid of dying. Was his faith in the living God not the straight and true thing he had believed it to be? Surely a man rightly adjusted in his relations with God would almost welcome death gladly as a way into the land of glory?

He took a turn on deck and looked at the other passengers. The English emigrants were shrieking with fear. But there were some who were apparently unaffected, even when the mainsail split with a crack of doom. On the contrary, they courageously sang hymns in a language that Wesley had gradually learnt to recognize. They were the Moravians leaving their fatherland, on an English ship bound for an uncertain future in the American colonies. These pilgrims of God were singing, quite unmoved, the songs of their faith and their childhood. The Germans had always been willing to undertake the most menial tasks on board, all those things that the others would not do. They insisted that it helped them to avoid the sin of pride. And now they were proving that even during a storm they were still strong Christian personalities. It was not only Wesley's inquiring mind that awoke, but his whole soul, his innermost self, clamoured to discover what it was the Germans had that he clearly lacked himself.

'Was you not afraid,' asked Wesley, when the storm had subsided.

'I thank God, no!' was the reply.

'But were not your women and children afraid?'

'No; our women and children are not afraid to die.'

Possibly the Germans could not compare with Wesley in the matter of Christian duty and scrupulous compliance with the law. Even the strictest Pharisee among them could not grudge Wesley the fact that he managed to keep all religious commandments and precepts so exactly. But here he had encountered something more—a way of life he could not claim as his own.

Wesley was deeply occupied at this time with thoughts about what things had been like in the early Christian Church. He and his friends studied the Bible daily and compared it with the writings of the Church fathers. And now here among these German Christians he thought that he saw again uniquely reincarnated the first Christian congregation. Later in life he said after attending the ordination of one of the Moravian bishops that sitting there I could 'forget the seventeen hundred years between, and imagine myself in one of those assemblies where form and state were not, but Paul the tent-maker or Peter the fisherman presided, yet with the demonstration of the Spirit and of power'.

Immediately after setting sail from England the two brothers had decided not to eat meat or drink wine, the staple diet at that period, but to live almost wholly on biscuits and rice. Later they decided to dispense with supper, too. Once after a storm Wesley's berth was soaked through, so he lay down to sleep on the deck. 'I believe I shall not find it needful to go to bed, as it is called, any more,' he remarked with ascetic joy at the possibility of being able to deny himself yet another of life's comforts.

On 6th February 1736 he set foot on American soil for the first time. The occasion is responsible for one of the extremely few descriptions of nature that we find in his *Journal*. Clearly Wesley was deeply moved by meeting spring at a time when in England it was still winter. After the passengers had landed Wesley gathered them all together on a hillside and there they knelt down and thanked God for a fair voyage and prayed for His defence in the future.

Oglethorpe now took a boat to Savannah and handed over his command and the responsibility for the emigrants to Wesley.

Re-sighting land had a different effect on the various people who had taken part in the voyage. The crew engaged in prolonged revelry. Wesley did not consider this the proper way to celebrate their arrival and with his own hand split open the kegs and allowed the rum to drain away. It is doubtful whether this increased his popularity with the crew.

In America Wesley got to know yet another German Moravian, namely August Gottlieb Spangenberg, who the year before had accompanied the first contingent of Germans to Georgia and who later became the leader of the whole Moravian Church. Wesley, who was always interested in his fellow men and particularly in the various sects of the Faith, asked Spangenberg how he could best behave in the new colony.

'Do you know yourself? Have you the witness within yourself?' Spangenberg asked. This was something that Samuel Wesley had spoken to him of on his death-bed—'The inward witness—that is . . . the strongest proof of Christianity.' An even more astonishing question followed: 'Do you know Jesus Christ?' Wesley hesitated a moment. Then he answered: 'I know He is the Saviour of the World.' 'True,' Spangenberg answered, 'But do you know He has saved you?' Wesley answered: 'I hope He has died to save me.' Then the German pastor asked him: 'Do you know yourself?' 'I do,' replied Wesley. But later he was forced to add: 'I fear they were vain words.'

While they were at anchor in the Savannah River, a chief of the people Wesley had come to help came on board. The Indian Tomo-Chachi had earlier been in England with Oglethorpe and had then aroused great respect and stimulated interest in Georgia. With him were some of his relatives, and their interpreter was an Indian woman who had married an Englishman. This is the speech of welcome Tomo-Chachi made to the four young missionaries:

'I am glad you are come. When I was in England, I desired that some would speak the Great Word to me; and my nation then desired to hear it. But since that time we have been all put into confusion. The French have built a fort with one hundred men in it in one place, and a fort with one hundred men in it in another. And the Spaniards are preparing for war. The English traders, too, put us into confusion, and have set our people against hearing the Great Word. For they speak with a double tongue; some say one thing of it and some another. Yet I am glad you are come. I will go up and speak to the wise men of our nation; and I hope they will hear. But we would not be made Christians as the Spaniards make Christians: we would be taught before we are baptized.'

Chapter VIII

Parish Minister in Georgia

WESLEY BEGAN his work as minister in Savannah on the 7th March 1736, by preaching on the text 1 Corinthians 13, the hymn of love. The reading for the day was Jesus' prediction of His treatment at the hands of the world. The courthouse where the meeting was held was packed with people. The previous minister had been given notice because he had married an Englishman to an Indian woman, and he had now left. It was in a mood of great expectation that the little community of colonists received their new minister. Wesley, however, considered the text of the day to be a bad omen:

'When I saw the number of people crowding into the church, the deep attention with which they received the word, and the seriousness that afterwards sat on all their faces, I could scarce refrain from giving the lie to experience and reason and Scripture all together. I could hardly believe that the greater, the far greater part of this attentive, serious people would hereafter trample underfoot that word, and say all manner of evil falsely of him that spake it.'

Savannah consisted at this period of about forty log houses that had been built by the first emigrants. In addition there were about a hundred or a hundred and fifty timber houses in the course of construction. There were five hundred and eighteen people in the town, great and small, and the whole of Wesley's parish comprised some seven hundred souls. There was no church in the town, and, as has been said, services were held in the courthouse, except when it was being used for some other purpose. The minister's house was one of the few large and roomy houses in the place, and visitors often stayed there. The house was situated on the outskirts of the town and surrounded by a garden.

That the new minister made a great impression was amply demonstrated by the fact that one of the leading families of the place had to cancel a ball it had arranged because no guests came. The minister, it happened, was holding a prayer-meeting at the same hour.

The first few days Wesley and his friends spent with the Germans, because the parsonage was not properly in order. Wesley had no words strong enough to praise their serious Christianity and enormous diligence.

The married immigrants from the *Simmonds* travelled with Oglethorpe down to Frederica, another colonial settlement about a hundred miles farther south on the coast. With them went Charles Wesley, who was Oglethorpe's secretary, and Benjamin Ingham, who was busily engaged in compiling an Indian dictionary. The only friend Wesley had in Savannah was Charles Delamotte, but he, by way of recompense, looked up to Wesley as though he were a prophet.

Wesley set about his work in Savannah with the greatest ardour. He read and studied perseveringly, particularly the history of the Primitive Church, and fixed himself up in a spartan and simple fashion in his new house. He had always been fond of gardening and relaxed from his work now and again by doing a turn in the rectory garden. His *Journal* relates how he repaired the path leading to the house, arranged his books, and wrote letters and sermons. But first and foremost he was priest-in-charge of a parish—of unusual dimensions, it is true—and he entertained dreams of creating a new Kingdom of God in accordance with the ideals of the Primitive Church here in this colonist community. He revived a number of customs of the early Church, and introduced them despite a growing indignation among his parishioners.

His first ecclesiastical duty in America was to baptize a child. The usual practice, of course, is to sprinkle water over the child's head, but Wesley immersed it completely three times. Earlier the child had been sick, 'but recovered from that hour', Wesley triumphantly adds. But not all the mothers were willing to risk this experiment. One mother comes to him with a child she wished to have baptized, but

'Neither Mr Parker nor I will consent to its being dipped.'

'If you "certify that" your "child is weak, it will suffice to pour water upon it".'

'Nay, the child is not weak; but I am resolved it shall not be dipped.' Wesley refused to baptize the child in these circumstances.

Wesley revived other rules that had gradually become disregarded. No one for instance was allowed to attend communion who had not given notice in advance. The Quakers and Dissenters, of whom there were many in the colony, had first to be baptized according to the ritual of the Anglican Church if they wished to borrow the church hall. Following the example of his father in Epworth, Wesley began to make house-to-house visits, exhorting, admonishing, reading, praying, and subjecting his congregation to a most stringent discipline. Yet despite all this, he was well liked in the town in this first period.

He also took notice of all the gossip that prevailed in the little, closed-in, colonial settlement. He used to tell all those concerned what this person or that had said about him or her. This he did with the best of intentions, wishing to have clear reports and acknowledged facts from which might be formed a real foundation for repentance. The principles of Oxford Methodism were not acceptable, however, to all the different minds collected here.

It was not long before trouble began to smoulder among the people, as it had done with his father in Epworth. But it was actually in the neighbouring town of Frederica that Wesley for the first time in his life experienced intrigue, malice, and wickedness on a large scale. A certain settler named Horton attacked the young clergyman openly.

'I like nothing you do. All your sermons are satires upon particular persons, therefore I will never hear you more; and all the people are of my mind, for we won't hear ourselves abused. Besides, they say they are Protestants. But as for you, they cannot tell what religion you are of. They never heard of such religion before. They do not know what to make of it. And then your private behaviour—all the quarrels that have been here since you came have been 'long of you. Indeed, there is neither man nor woman in the town who minds a word you say. And so you may preach long enough; but nobody will come to hear you.'

Wesley's resuscitation of the precepts of the early Church was regarded as the introduction of a new religion, and his well-meant candour caused quarrels among his parishioners of whom Horton was the most implacable enemy Wesley had in the colony.

John was not the only one who got into difficulties. Benjamin Ingham had come with a letter from Charles that sounded like the despairing cry of a drowning man. John immediately set out for Frederica and Ingham remained behind in Savannah to look after the parish there.

When John reached Frederica, after a perilous journey, he found his brother in the depth of despair. He had not only managed to become thoroughly unpopular with the townfolk but had also fallen into disgrace with Oglethorpe. In addition to this he had contracted influenza, but his spirits revived when he caught sight of John.

It was Mrs Hawkins and another person who had made things difficult for Charles. On board the *Simmonds*, Charles had opposed her being allowed to take part in communion because he considered her a hypocrite. Now the woman took revenge on Charles in such a refined manner that her behaviour seemed like the product of a warped mind.

Oglethorpe was a handsome man but reputed to be insensible to feminine charms. On some pretext or another, therefore, the women went to Charles and confessed with feigned remorse that they had had an illicit affair with the governor! To complete the business they then approached the governor and confessed that they had had an illicit affair with Charles! It was only fear of scandal and of undermining the esteem of the official class that prevented Oglethorpe from 'exposing' Charles. But in the meantime relations became very strained between the governor and his secretary.

Oglethorpe, however, had more important things to do than finding out the rights and wrongs of items of malicious gossip. It looked as though there would be war with the Spaniards who had garrisons not far away. He would have to put the colony in a state of preparedness, particularly as the fort he occupied was situated on Spanish territory.

John alone was capable of sorting out the personal entanglements in Frederica. Oglethorpe preserved throughout his life a reverent respect for John Wesley, and when the general and empire builder met the diminutive churchman later in life, he bowed his head respectfully. There is no doubt that John saved Oglethorpe's reputation and career, and possibly his own and Charles Wesley's life too.

When the tangle in Frederica had been straightened out, Wesley returned to Savannah. Properly speaking he was a missionary to the Indians with a salary of fifty pounds a year, but it proved difficult to make a start with his work among the Indians. Oglethorpe was the stumbling-block. He feared unrest among the Indians if these zealous and inflexible missionaries were to get to work among them, and apart from this he needed the four Oxford men to take part in the government of the colony, as officials working among the white population.

For this reason Wesley decided to spend still more time on the 'little flock'. He and the more serious Christians shared the idea that they should form a 'society', which would meet once or twice a week and enable them to reprove, instruct, and exhort one another. Out of those who came together in this way, a smaller number was chosen to meet every Sunday evening to further the work of attaining salvation and holiness. Here we have the prototype or at least one of the models, for Methodism's class-meetings and chosen groups or 'Select Bands'.

At the same time Wesley began diligently to study the treasury of German hymns that had been opened for him by the Moravians. He translated many of these hymns, sang them himself and tried them out at the meetings of the society, introducing thereby a whole new feature into Anglican Church life. It is noteworthy that even though it was Charles who was destined to become Methodism's great hymnist, here too, it was John who showed the way and was the originator of what has been called a revolution in British hymnology. He also taught himself Spanish and translated at least one psalm from Spanish in this period.

Charles Delamotte conducted a school in the village for the children—about forty of them—and Wesley catechized them in church on Sundays. A story is related about Wesley's attitude towards the heartless snobbery that was beginning to make its insidious appearance among the settlers. One of the children had no shoes and was pitilessly teased by the other children. Next day Wesley himself took over the instruction, and confronted the school—barefoot! From that moment there was an end to the teasing, and Wesley had found a little friend for life.

Meanwhile, matters were going from bad to worse in Frederica. One day Charles turned up in Savannah and refused to go back. Shortly afterwards he returned to England.

It was a trifling affair that had put Charles to flight. A letter he had written to his brother had been opened and read. In the letter Charles had used a few Greek words to characterize some of the town's ladies. No one in the colony except the Oxford Methodists could read Greek. One and all of the town's womenfolk felt themselves insulted and their reputation challenged. One possibility alone remained; retreat to Old England!

John now travelled back and forth between the two places to take charge of both parishes. After a particularly fatiguing journey he made his way to Frederica, sick and ailing, and sought out Dr Hawkins. The doctor was not at home, but his wife was. Mrs Hawkins had hitherto always liked John Wesley. She had played the penitent when he had admonished her, had been 'open', and 'much affected', as he recorded in his private diary.

On this occasion, too, conversation started peacefully enough. He was requested to take a seat, and the conversation touched upon his brother's famous letter. When Wesley upbraided Mrs Hawkins for her interest in the matter, she started up and said Wesley was a 'scoundrel', 'a villain', 'a pitiful rascal', and various other things of the same nature. At that moment the doctor himself appeared. When he heard that the Greek words in the letter referred to his wife, they both attacked Wesley with abuse and curses. Wesley could not restrain his tears. 'I know not whether they interpreted this as fear; but they rose in their language, and told me they would uncase [i.e. unfrock] us both.'

Oglethorpe tried to mediate in the quarrel, but without success. Not without humour Wesley tells of a characterization that his enemy Horton gave him: Horton thought Wesley delighted in doing mischief. 'I believe, in a morning when you say your prayers, you resolve against it; but by the time you have been abroad two hours, all your resolutions are vanished, and you can't be easy till you're at it again.'

Mrs Hawkins sent her servant to fetch Wesley. He replied that if one of his parishioners sent for him, it was his duty to go. But he insisted that the servant should be present. When Wesley entered he sat down on the edge of the bed. Mrs Hawkins was standing a little distance away with her hands behind her back. 'Sir,' she said threateningly, 'you have wronged me, and I will shoot you through the head this moment with a brace of balls.' Thereupon she brought forth a pistol and aimed it at his head. Wesley took hold of the pistol to wrest it from her, but in her other hand she had a pair of scissors and now she threw herself upon him with all her weight and forced him down upon the bed, shouting either she would have his hair or see his heart-blood, and cursing foully all the time. Wesley could hardly call for help in a situation as compromising as this. The servant came in but did not lift a finger in his defence. Soon a constable arrived and the doctor himself. Encouraged by her husband the fury found new courage, and she took hold of Wesley's cassock in her teeth and tore off the sleeve.

Wesley went to the Governor and told him all that had happened to him. He had no wish to hurt anyone, he said, but on the other hand he had to protect his own honour.

In the end a sort of agreement was reached whereby they should not speak to one another any more, a cause of great thankfulness to Wesley. 'Blessed be God who hath at length given me a full discharge, in the sight of men and angels, from all intercourse with one "whose heart is snares and knots and her hands as bands".' This difficulty had been removed from his path, but the way that lay ahead was to take him through high places and deep waters—here in Savannah he was to find his great love.

Chapter IX

Wesley's Great Love

IN THE words of a modern description, Wesley at thirty-three was 'a beautiful little man, under the medium height like all the Wesleys, very slender and spare of body, but so justly-proportioned that his lack of height wore the aspect of an added grace. In company with larger men, he compared as might a rapier against a sword. He wore his dark hair rather long, curling slightly at the ends, and brushed to a burnished glossiness. His large, dark-blue eyes had that clear, cold light which expresses will and the autocratic intellect; for he had not yet attained the sweet patience which made his later years so gracious. . . . His clothes . . . were spinsterishly neat.'

He was strong and manly, often took long walking tours sleeping overnight under the stars, swam in the river, and worked regularly and cheerfully in the rectory garden.

Such was the Wesley the Governor thought so highly of, and whom he was desirous of attaching to the colony for good. If only they could induce the young minister to marry, he would then want to settle down permanently in Georgia.

The wife of the magistrate, Mrs Causton, had a niece called Sophia (Sophy) Christina Hopkey. Time was to prove that this magistrate was not an honest man, but Miss Sophy, to judge from all appearances, would make a good wife for Wesley. She was young, pretty, and intelligent. She had, however, one suitor already, of so-called good family, but he was so wild and violent that Miss Sophy had not ventured to associate with him. But he had sworn he would have her. 'If anyone comes between us, there will be a funeral instead of a wedding,' he had threatened.

We have seen how Wesley had already had his share of youthful love-affairs, enthusiasms, and disappointments. But always he drew back as though he had an unconscious feeling that marriage would hinder him in his great calling.

Wesley thrived in the company of women. Yet he was far from being frivolous. He mixed with women because they listened to him devotedly and receptively when he read to them or discussed spiritual matters, but he was always surprised and disappointed when it turned out after a time that their admiration was not content to stop there.

With the exception of a few women he had got to know on board the

Simmonds, all Wesley's female acquaintances were highly educated people. This applied equally to his mother and to his sisters, who admired him and loved him. Now, however, he was about to fall deeply in love with a woman who was completely different from any he had met before.

Dr J. E. Rattenbury says of Wesley's love for Sophy Hopkey: 'No experiences of John Wesley give us so vivid a realization of his humanness as the Georgia love episode. His love of Grace Murray in later days and his bitter disappointment was in many ways a similar episode, but his feeling about her as a helpmeet in his work as well as a wife lessens, to some extent, the humanity of the story.'

Here is a description Wesley gives of Sophy Hopkey after he had returned to England. Sitting once more in his bachelor quarters in Oxford, he looked back upon the storms that had passed over his soul. He was writing to evaluate, to forget, and to set aside, but also to let his mother know what he had experienced. He headed the manuscript with the characteristic title: 'Snatched as a brand out of the fire.'

'She was eighteen years old. And from the beginning of our intimate acquaintance till this day, I verily believe she used no guile: not only because even now I know no instance to the contrary, nor only because the simplicity of her behaviour was a constant voucher for her sincerity; but because of the entire openness of all her conversation, answering whatever questions I proposed, without either hesitation or reserve, immediately and directly. Another thing I was much pleased with in her was, that whenever we were conversing or reading, there was such a stillness in her whole behaviour, scarce stirring hand or foot, that "she seemed to be, all but her attention, dead".'

There is little doubt that she did her utmost to please this strange minister who was as different from her first suitor as the day from the night. She did everything she could to make a good impression. She knew that he didn't care for trinkets and finery, so she didn't wear them. But how did he like women to be dressed? She asked Oglethorpe, who answered with military abruptness and without reflection: 'In white gowns.' So Sophy wore a white gown when she came to prayer-meetings in the parsonage at five o'clock in the morning, when later in the day she came to read French with the minister, or when ever more frequently she came to lunch with Wesley and Delamotte, who became more and more disquieted about the state of affairs.

Both the governor and the magistrate were delighted by this development. The magistrate took Wesley riding with him and showed him the family's great possessions. Sophy was heiress to all the family's wealth and was not completely poverty-stricken herself.

But if everything augured well for a brilliant match, there were still obstacles to overcome. These obstacles lay in Wesley's own mind.

One of the Holy Club's ideals was that the members should remain single, and had not Paul also recommended this state for a servant of the Lord? In addition he ought as soon as possible to travel inland to the Indians, and he could hardly take Sophy with him there. Finally, he had once said that he had no mind to get married, and he believed he had meant it seriously.

Life at the Caustons was not always very easy for Sophy so she sometimes made a trip to Frederica. After Charles had returned to England, Wesley, too, had to go there now and again. He went to the Caustons one day and asked if he could take her a greeting from them. Causton stared thoughtfully in front of him and said: 'The girl will never be easy till she is married.' 'But she is too much afflicted to have a thought of it,' objected Wesley. Causton wasn't quite so sure about that. If he could but find her an honest and good man, then there would be no difficulty about financial arrangements. 'I give her up to you,' he said. 'Do what you will with her. Take her into your own hands. Promise her what you will. I will make it good.'

When Wesley arrived in Frederica he saw that everything he had built up there had collapsed again. No morning or evening prayers were being held any longer, and even Sophy had begun to show a decided slackness. Spiritually she was not a shadow of her former self. A whole string of her good intentions had been forgotten. She no longer fasted, and she even entertained the idea of travelling back to England. Wesley did everything he could to dissuade her from such a step. He read her some of the most arresting passages from Law's *Serious Call to a Devout and Holy Life*, but nothing seemed to help. 'I was at first a little surprised and discouraged,' he said, 'but I soon recollected my spirits and remembered my calling and the words which cannot fail: "Greater is He that is in you than he that is in the world".'

In the middle of his hard work of winning souls he managed to find time for repeated visits to Sophy to try to dissuade her from going. He employed one argument after another but to no avail. Finally he appealed to the friendship they had for one another and the girl confessed with tears; 'Now my resolution begins to stagger.'

Meantime, a knot appeared in the thread that united Oglethorpe and Wesley. The governor ignored him completely on one occasion. Wesley had expected such a development, and he was distressed about it, not primarily for his own sake, but because now he was no longer in a position to help Sophy out of her difficulties with the Caustons. Well, she would just have to travel back to England again.

But now she had changed her mind. 'I will not stir a foot. . . . Let him [Mr Oglethorpe] be pleased or displeased. I care not. Sir, you encouraged me in my greatest trials. Be not discouraged in your own. . . . If Mr Oglethorpe will not, God will help you.'

Oglethorpe decided that Sophy must now return to Savannah. 'She can go in none [i.e. boat] but yours, and indeed there is none so proper,' he said.

Wesley began to realize that there was a conspiracy against his bachelorhood. But he would not have been John Wesley if he had not sat down and systematically arranged all the reasons that proved that everything would still, perhaps, be all right. 'I saw the danger to myself but yet had a good hope I should be delivered out of it, (1) because it was not my choice which brought me into it; (2) because I still felt in myself the same desire and design to live a single life; and (3) because I was persuaded should my desire and design be changed, yet her resolution to live single would continue.'

Oglethorpe arranged things so that they were the only passengers on board. Nothing was to be neglected that would make 'the wish and the plan' to remain single as difficult as possible. About noon one beautiful October day, the boat got under way. Wesley utilized the larger part of the first few days reading aloud to Sophy from Fleury's *Histoire Ecclésiastique*, 'a book I chose for her sake chiefly, as setting before her such glorious examples of truth and patience, in the sufferings of those ancient worthies, "who resisted unto blood, striving against sin".'

In the evening they landed for the night. To keep out the night-dew they made a tent with the mainsail fastened to four poles. The night was cold, but Sophy 'complained of nothing, appearing as satisfied as if she had been warm upon a bed of down'. Wesley could not forbear admiring her seriousness and charm. She certainly did all she could to please this man, whose every thought seemed to be concerned with Christian holiness. He recorded their 'close conversation' on this subject. 'The openness with which she owned her ignorance of it, and the earnest desire she showed for fresh instruction, as it much endeared her to me, so it made me hope she would one day prove an eminent pattern of it.'

One night, when sleep eluded him, Wesley found Sophy also awake. Turning impulsively to her, he exclaimed: 'Miss Sophy, I should think myself happy if I was to spend my life with you.' He said later that this was 'the expression of a sudden wish, not of any primed design'.

Sophy began to cry and protested that she was very unhappy, for she wasn't going to have Tommy, who was a bad man, and yet she couldn't accept anyone else. 'Sir, you don't know the danger you are in. I beg you would speak no word more on this head.' Then she added after a little while: 'When others have spoken to me on the subject, I felt an aversion to them. But I don't feel any to you. We may converse on other subjects as freely as ever.' The singing of a psalm sealed the close of their conversation.

The journey was nearing its end, and Sophy was thinking with horror about the prospect of having to live with the Caustons again. Here her new-won resolve to lead a pious life would be subjected to severe trial. Wesley offered her a room at the parsonage. 'Or, which I think would be best of all . . . you may live in the house with the Germans,' he added, after having thought about it for a while. To this offer she made no reply.

After the journey to Frederica, Sophy came to him every day to read French and devotional literature. One day Wesley again hinted at the possibility of marriage. 'Indeed it was only a sudden thought, which had not the consent of my own mind. Yet I firmly believe, had she closed with me at that time, my judgement would have made but a faint resistance.'

But Sophy considered it more fitting for a minister to remain unmarried and without worldly cares. She herself would also prefer to remain single, she said, and her friend 'used no argument to induce her to alter her resolution'.

However, thoughts of marriage continued to engage him more and more. The German pastor, Töltschig, whom he had asked for advice, could not see any reason why Wesley should not marry Sophy. After this conversation, Wesley returned home 'amazed to the last degree'.

He thought over the advice he had received from Ingham and Delamotte, but they were far from agreeing with the German. How would Wesley be sure of Sophy's sincerity? Was he sure that her piety wasn't just a blind? And was he sure of his own feelings? They advised him to leave the town for a while to analyse his real emotions.

Wesley followed this advice, but first he sent this little letter to Sophy:

'Feb. 6. I find, Miss Sophy, I can't take fire into my bosom, and not be burnt. I am therefore retiring for a while to desire the direction of God. Join with me, my friend, in fervent prayer, that He would show me what is best to be done.'

The following day he had to go to Savannah. He remained there but one hour. 'My heart was with Miss Sophy all the time. I longed to see her, were it but for a moment. And when I was called to take boat, it was as the sentence of death; but believing it was the call of God, I obeyed. . . . I instantly cried to God for resignation. And I found that and peace together. I said, "Sure it is a dream". I was in a new world. The change was as from death to life. I went back to Irene [a place] wondering and rejoicing.'

When some time later he came back to Savannah, Sophy said to him: 'People wonder what I can do so long at your house; I am resolved not to breakfast with you any more. And I won't come to you any more alone.'

Next day, she suspended her French lessons, though inviting him to come to her home whenever he might wish to do so. Wesley answered: 'You know, Miss Sophy, I don't love a crowd, and there is always one there.' To this Sophy encouragingly replied: 'But we needn't be in it.'

Wesley fought an earnest battle with himself as he felt himself continually being drawn like a magnet to the house where Sophy lived. There was one person who looked upon it all with mounting grief, namely Charles Delamotte. He admired Wesley with the enthusiasm of youth and worshipped him as a hero. Weeping he told Wesley he found that they must part, for he could not live in that house when Wesley was married to Miss Sophy. John told him, 'I had no intention to marry her', but Delamotte was convinced that Wesley did not know his own heart.

They decided to settle this serious matter by appealing to God direct. This was done by drawing lots. On slips of paper they wrote: 'Marry', 'Think not of it this year', 'Think of it no more'. After they had prayed to God, Delamotte drew a slip. Time stood still as he slowly unrolled it. There it stood: 'Think of it no more'. Instead of being crushed, Wesley burst out gladly: 'Thy will be done!' They drew once more to decide whether or not Wesley ought ever to speak with Sophy again. On the piece they drew it read: 'Only in the presence of Mr Delamotte.' Wesley was able to accept this, too, and give thanks to God.

But his battle was far from being over, for now rivals began to appear. A few days later Sophy was again lunching at the rectory, and in Delamotte's presence Wesley questioned Sophy.

'I hear Mr Williamson pays his addresses to you. Is it true?' 'If it were not I would have told you so. . . . I shall never deceive you. . . . Of one thing, sir, be assured: I will never take any step in anything of importance without first consulting you.'

On the following day Wesley was again visiting the Caustons. The lady welcomed him in and said: 'Sir, Mr Causton and I are exceedingly obliged to you for all the pains you have taken about Sophy. And so is Sophy, too; and she desires you would publish the banns of marriage between her and Mr Williamson on Sunday.'

Seeing him stunned by the news she added: 'Sir, you don't seem to be well pleased. Have you any objection to it?' Bewilderment was uppermost in Wesley's mind. 'Madam, I don't seem to be awake. Surely I am in a dream.' Mrs Causton explained that the engagement had taken place after Wesley had left them the evening before. 'Afterwards Mr Williamson asked Mr Causton's and my consent, which we gave him; but if you have any objection to it, pray speak,' she urged. 'Speak to her . . . go to her. She will be very glad to hear anything Mr Wesley has to say.' Wisely he refused. 'If Miss Sophy is engaged, I have nothing to say.'

His first need was to go home and lay this before his Heavenly

Father and then to discuss it with his friend, Delamotte. An hour later he was again at the Caustons, where he found Sophy with her fiancé. There was a painful silence when Wesley entered. Williamson broke the silence and said:

'I suppose, sir, you know what was agreed on last night between Miss Sophy and me?' 'I have heard something,' he replied, 'but I could not believe it, unless I should hear it from Miss Sophy herself.' The assurance was given him, but with a qualification, as Sophy told him: 'Sir, I have given Mr Williamson my consent—unless you have anything to object.'

The thought suddenly struck him: 'What if she means, unless you will marry me?' But he told himself that she who was so honest would have said so straight out if she had intended it. 'No,' he answered. 'If you have given your consent, the time is past; I have nothing to object.'

Williamson now took his leave so that they could talk it out together. There were tears and emotion on both sides. As soon as Wesley was able to speak, he reminded her of her resolution, 'If she married at all, to marry none but a religious man', and desired her to consider whether Mr Williamson was such. She said, 'She had no proof to the contrary. . . . I no otherwise consented, than if you had nothing to object.'

'I sat there with the words on my tongue,' Wesley said later. "Miss Sophy, will you marry me?" ' For the rest of his life he wondered why he never uttered this decisive question. His whole being was in a turmoil. He was afraid lest her lot should be unhappiness and misery, and he also thought that he himself was somewhat to be pitied. But out of deference to God's will he held back.

'I hope I shall always have your friendship,' Sophy said, as Wesley rose to take his leave. 'I can still be your friend, though I should not stay in America.' 'But I hope you won't leave us.' 'I can't at all judge how God will dispose of me.' 'However, you will let me have your correspondence?' 'I doubt it cannot be,' he concluded, and exhorting them both to remember what he had taught them, he kissed them and took his leave of Sophy as though he were never going to see her again.

At home, sunk in despair, he tried to pray but was lost in pain and confusion. Little relief was found in talk with Delamotte, and further perplexity added by a visit from Mr Causton who said that he did not approve of the match and had neither denied nor given his consent. He could not understand how Wesley could have let Sophy slip from his grasp and told him that if he pleased, he might have her still—'but if you won't, another will.'

Sophy came to evening prayers at the Parsonage and stayed behind while her fiancé walked restlessly up and down outside. Within, John was earnestly questioning the girl. 'Miss Sophy, you said yesterday you would take no steps—anything of importance—without first consulting me.'

She answered seriously and repeated several times: 'Why, what could I do? I can't live in that house. I can't bear these shocks. . . . I have no particular inclination for Mr Williamson. I only promised if no objection appeared. But what can I do?'

Unresolved her perplexities had to remain, for Williamson, frightened of leaving her any longer in conversation with Wesley, came in to fetch his future bride and they departed. Wesley could only exclaim in his secret diary:

'No such day since I first saw the sun!
O deal tenderly with Thy servant!
Let me not see such another.'

Early next morning Wesley was again outside Causton's house knocking at the door, anxious to find out whether Sophy's decision was indeed final. It was Williamson who met him by the door. With a little irritation he said: 'Sir, you shall speak with her no more till we are married. You can persuade her to anything. After you went from the Lot yesterday, she would neither eat nor drink for two hours; but was crying continually, and in such an agony she was fit for nothing.'

Wesley replied that Williamson would be able to make Miss Sophy's decisions for her later, but today she was still her own mistress. He then asked Sophy if she were still sticking to her decision. She answered, 'Yes'. He then exhorted them to publish the banns in lawful fashion and to love one another in the fear of God, and then heavy of heart, he went home to yet another day of pain and anguish.

The next day the newly-engaged couple travelled to another town and were married a few days later, on 12th March 1737—one year to the day after Wesley first set eyes on his dearly-loved Sophy. A year later, on 12th March 1738, he completed his written account of this love-affair—'An affair with Miss Sophy Hopkey', and inscribed upon the blank outside leaf: 'Snatched as a brand out of the fire.'

We who read this record nowadays can trace influences upon the subconscious provided by the experiences of early childhood. We see Susanna Wesley's gentle and determined figure behind her son during the whole period. It was she who had imprinted upon his mind a love of God's will. Her child was to seek God's kingdom before all else even if it meant cutting across what the world calls good fortune. We may consider the sacrifice was surely too great. But if Wesley had married Sophy Hopkey, he would probably have become a persevering but comparatively commonplace parish minister in Georgia—not the messenger of God for his age. Future events proved that he acted rightly.

The newly-weds soon returned and Wesley noticed with horror how 'Miss Sophy', as he still obstinately calls her in his journal, had become lax in her spiritual life. She failed to attend the prayer-meetings at five o'clock in the morning and ceased fasting. This would not have been so bad in others, but Wesley felt it deeply when it concerned her. It looks as if Wesley now for a time lost his sound power of judgement. He upbraided Sophy for several faults in her behaviour and had numerous clashes with her. On Mrs Causton's advice he writes a long letter to 'Miss Sophy', in which all his grievances and complaints are put down clearly and methodically. He begs her to admit her mistakes and then all will be forgiven. It appears, however, that she feels no urge to do this, for no answer arrives.

The summer passes in study and vigorous parochial work. There is constant murmuring against Wesley in the parish. The atmosphere is charged. But there is no serious outbreak until Sunday, 7th August 1737, when the following entry appears in the *Journal:*

'I repelled Mrs Williamson from the Holy Communion for the reasons specified in my letter of July 5, as well as for not giving me notice of her design to communicate after having intermitted it for some time. I foresaw the consequences well, but remembered the promise in the Epistle for the day, "God is faithful, who will not suffer you to be tempted above that ye are able; but will with the temptation also make a way to escape, that ye may be able to bear it". '

Nor were the consequences long in coming. The very next day Causton obtained a warrant for Wesley's arrest for defaming the character of Mrs Williamson without any cause by refusing to administer to her the Sacrament of the Lord's Supper, in a public congregation. The order stipulated that Wesley could pay bail to avoid arrest, but the judge said, 'Sir, Mr Wesley's word is sufficient', and he was permitted to leave the court.

Undisturbed he took up his ministry again. Doors were slammed in his face as he went visiting from house to house, but indefatigably he carried on. He held services and prayer-meetings even though only a handful of people came—all while the critical court action was being prepared in which Wesley's case was to be tried.

The jury was to consist of forty-four men, the so-called 'grand jury'. It included, however, a Frenchman who did not understand English, a Roman Catholic, an atheist, and seventeen Dissenters, who were thus to be put into a position to decide questions concerning the organization of the Anglican Church.

The case for the prosecution against Wesley is said to be one of the strangest that ever came before a British court. All sorts of complaints had emerged. In addition to his having written to Mrs Williamson after her marriage—at the instigation of her aunt, we remember—was included the fact that he had refused to baptize a child without immersion, that he had refused to read the burial service at a certain person's death, that he had refused to allow someone to be a godfather because the person in question had not received communion, and so on. Among the charges was of course the fact that he had turned Mrs Williamson away from the communion-table.

Wesley insisted that he had written to Mrs Williamson merely in the capacity of minister and then at the prompting of her aunt. As for the other charges, he refused to answer them before a lay court, since he thought they concerned ecclesiastical questions which ought to be decided only by the Church authorities. Nevertheless, he was found guilty, after astonishing judicial proceedings involving six sittings during which Wesley was refused the right to offer any defence.

Wesley realized now that for the time being his sojourn in America was over. He announced his intention of returning to England by posting up a scrap of paper saying that all those who had borrowed books from him must bring them back because he was leaving for England. A half-hearted attempt was made by his congregation to dissuade him, but at heart they were only too glad to be rid of this dauntless chastiser.

After several eventful experiences, Wesley reached the coast and went on board the ship *Samuel*. It was not his intention to leave America for good; both he and Charles, who had travelled home a year before, entertained plans for returning.

Rattenbury makes the following pertinent observation about Wesley as he was in Georgia: 'He reminds one at this time more than once of Ibsen's Brand, that hard and heroic soul, who was ultimately chased by his exasperated parishioners out of his parish into the grim Norwegian mountains. So the Georgians drove Wesley to the ocean.'

The return journey was stormy again and Wesley realized to his shame his unwillingness to die yet. He saw himself in a very gloomy light and for several days was unable to speak to anyone about God—something quite unique in Wesley's life. But he soon recovered and began the instruction of a young negro boy and a Frenchman who spoke no English.

On 1st February 1738 they reached Deal in England. The evening before, George Whitefield, later to supersede the brothers Wesley in popularity in America, had left for that country in response to John's plea for help.

Wesley's years in Georgia had been trying and difficult. He felt himself bound to High Church laws and decrees and imposed on people heavy burdens that he, too, tried with all his might to bear. During this period he learnt several foreign languages, published some scholarly works and wrote many of his finest sermons and best hymns. But the most important thing was that here in this unfinished colonial settlement he reaped a harvest of experience as an active parish minister and administrator, and he got to know his own limitations.

Chapter X

A Year of Grace

THE 7th February 1738 was for Wesley 'a day to be remembered'. On that day he met a man who was to help him out of the slavery of occupational piety into the glorious freedom of one of God's children. Once again it was a member of the German Moravian Brethren who came into his life—as Nitschmann, Töltschig, and Spangenberg had done earlier. This new representative of the Brotherhood was called Peter Böhler.

Böhler was nine years younger than Wesley. As a student in Jena in Germany he had come under the influence of German pietism, and from that time forth had delved deeper and deeper into the religion of experience. When later he met Count Zinzendorf he was attracted by the ideas and practices of the Brotherhood and joined it. Hitherto he had been a minister in the State Church, but now he transferred his activities to the Brethren. When Wesley met him in London he was on his way to America where he and several of his travelling companions intended to organize a mission among the negroes of Georgia. During their stay in London Wesley looked after his new-found friends.

Wesley preached at a number of churches during this time, but something made him doubt whether he would ever preach there again. After having conferred with General Oglethorpe, who happened to be in London, and various trustees of the colonies, he set off for Oxford with Peter Böhler who sighed over his ignorance of salvation by faith. 'My brother, my brother, that philosophy of yours must be purged away.'

The Holy Club had shrunk almost to nothing during his absence and his journey next took him to his mother. He needed to have a long talk with her.

Susanna Wesley lived with her dissolute son-in-law, Westley Hall, and her daughter, Martha, near Salisbury. Here Wesley found his mother again. We don't know what the two talked about, but he did not remain there long. The next day he was to set off to Tiverton, where his eldest brother, Samuel, was Headmaster of Blundell's School, but just as he was about to start, a message arrived from Oxford, saying that his brother Charles was mortally ill. So he had to go there instead.

Apparently Charles's pleurisy was much better when John reached him. Peter Böhler was there sitting with him, and John, who was now convinced he did not possess the faith to justify his continuing to preach, said despairingly to Böhler, that he was going to give it up. To this Böhler made this wise reply: 'Preach faith *till* you have it, and then, *because* you have it, you *will* preach faith.'

This advice Wesley followed. Not long after we find him visiting a prison to preach to the prisoners. Earlier he had rejected out of hand the idea of death-bed conversion. At that time conversion meant for him a long process that prisoners condemned to death could scarcely hope to live long enough to complete. Now, however, he preached the doctrine of conversion by faith alone to the prisoner Clifford, who gained salvation and experienced justification by faith alone long before Wesley himself had had this experience.

That conversion could take place in a moment filled him with ever-mounting surprise. 'I could not understand how this faith should be given in a moment: how a man could *at once* be thus turned from darkness to light, from sin and misery to righteousness and joy in the Holy Ghost. I searched the Scriptures again touching this very thing, particularly the Acts of the Apostles: but, to my utter astonishment, found scarce any instances there of other than *instantaneous* conversions; scarce any so slow as that of St Paul, who was three days in the pangs of the new birth.'

Biblical statistics thus seemed clear enough. But Wesley still had his objections: '*Thus*, I grant, God wrought in the *first* ages of Christianity; but the times are changed. What reason have I to believe He works in the same manner now?'

But on the following Sunday he was driven from this entrenchment also, for on this day Peter Böhler and four of his English Moravians came to see him. They were living witnesses that God in the space of a moment had delivered them from sin and fear to godliness and happiness—simply by faith in Jesus' blood. 'Here ended my disputing. I could now only cry out, "Lord, help Thou my unbelief!" ' When at the end these members of the United Brethren sang a psalm about full surrender into the hands of the Lord, the tears ran down Wesley's cheeks. He began to realize that the light of revelation was very near to him now.

Charles had now come to London himself, and John met him again on 1st May 1738 at the home of one of their friends, James Hutton. Hutton had been converted by a sermon Wesley had preached at his father's house in Westminster, and had originally wanted to go with them to Georgia. Now they met again, and on 1st May a little religious group or society was founded, later becoming known as 'The Fetter Lane Society', because it met in that place. Again it was Böhler who led the way, and the rules for the society were partly derived from Herrnhuter sources.

The so-called religious societies had been introduced into England by a German-born parson called Horneck at the close of the seventeenth century and they played a great rôle in the life of the time. They were often attacked by the Church, but Wesley had always had a sympathy with this kind of Christian activity. He had himself founded something of the sort in Savannah, and from the very beginning he was one of the leaders of the group in Fetter Lane.

The society was neither Methodist nor Moravian. The members had to profess Anglicanism. The rules required them to confess their sins to one another and to pray for one another. The members were divided into groups or 'bands' of from five to ten. At each meeting every single one of the members was expected to speak 'as freely, plainly, and concisely as he can, the real state of his heart, with his several temptations and deliverances, since the last time of meeting'. There were rules about the probationary period, special prayer days, and the love-feasts of the early Church.

Then 24th May 1738 dawned—the day when the clear light of the gospel broke through all Wesley's subservience to rules and philosophizing. He accepted salvation like a little child—without particularly deserving it and without being able fully to understand what had happened to him.

Many are the dissertations that have been written about what happened that day. Some have called it Wesley's conversion. We should note that Charles used this word to denote a corresponding experience that he had had three days earlier.

After Wesley had described the whole of his life, with its pitiless seeking after truth item by item right up to this time, the *Journal* continues:

'I continued thus to seek [faith] (though with strange indifference, dullness, and coldness, and unusually frequent relapses into sin) till Wednesday, May 24. I think it was about five this morning, that I opened my Testament on those words, . . . "There are given unto us exceeding great and precious promises, even that ye should be partakers of the divine nature". Just as I went out, I opened it again on those words, "Thou art not far from the kingdom of God". In the afternoon I was asked to go to St Paul's. The anthem was, "Out of the deep have I called unto Thee, O Lord: Lord, hear my voice. O let Thine ears consider well the voice of my complaint. If Thou, Lord, will be extreme to mark what is done amiss, O Lord, who may abide it? For there is mercy with Thee; therefore shalt Thou be feared. O Israel, trust in the Lord: for with the Lord there is mercy, and with Him is plenteous redemption. And he shall redeem Israel from all his sins."

'In the evening I went very unwillingly to a society in Aldersgate

Street, where one was reading Luther's preface to the Epistle to the Romans. About a quarter before nine, while he was describing the change which God works in the heart through faith in Christ, I felt my heart strangely warmed. I felt I did trust in Christ, Christ alone for salvation; and an assurance was given me that He had taken away *my* sins, even *mine*, and saved *me* from the law of sin and death.

'I began to pray with all my might for those who had in a more especial manner despitefully used me and persecuted me. I then testified openly to all there what I now first felt in my heart. But it was not long before the enemy suggested, "This cannot be faith; for where is thy joy?" Then was I taught that peace and victory over sin are essential to faith in the Captain of our salvation; but that, as to the transports of joy that usually attend the beginning of it, especially in those who have mourned deeply, God sometimes giveth, sometimes withholdeth them, according to the counsels of His own will.'

The period that followed was filled with crises and conflicts. It took time for Wesley to learn to live a life of faith. Now it was no longer Christ *and* good works that would save him, but Christ alone.

As early as 1725 Wesley had already made his decision to live his life in the service of God. The new world that opened before him after his 'evangelical conversion' symbolized for him a miraculous experience. Charles had had the same experience a few days before, Whitefield still earlier. Now the day of grace had arrived for John Wesley—Methodists the world over attach to this event an overwhelming importance. This is not the place to discuss what theological designation best describes this experience. For Wesley himself, at any rate, it meant a colossal change—outwardly as well as inwardly.

Wesley felt a deep thankfulness stream through his whole being. His gratitude was directed not least towards the movement that had opened his eyes to this newly-won kingdom of the soul, namely the Moravian Brethren. It was quite natural, therefore, that he should now redeem an old promise he had made himself: to travel to Germany and see what wonderful things God had done for those who worshipped Him in Count Zinzendorf's Herrnhut.

The Herrnhuters were also called the United Brethren or Moravian Brethren because the founders of the movement were German Lutheran Christians who had fled from Moravia to escape Catholic persecution and had established a refuge in Germany. It was the gifted and pious Count Zinzendorf who became the movement's great and unifying name. The Count was three years older than Wesley but died as early as 1760. Right from his earliest years he had been moved by strong religious yearnings and had been brought up in a strongly pietistic atmosphere. During a communion service in pietism's stronghold, Halle, he had experienced conversion. When he was studying law later in Wittenberg he also came to see the strong points in orthodoxy and with his sense for extracting the best from all the movements he came in contact with, he realized that the true basis of orthodoxy was salvation through grace. This later became the central theme of his own preaching.

Zinzendorf had the ambition to create a bright and warm religion of the heart. A Christian ought to be happy. The feeling of happiness was the great aim and broadly speaking the sign that proved one was a Christian. Zinzendorf was possessed of great talents as an organizer and leader. His guiding thought was the creation of small circles of believers divided into classes of married and unmarried, women and men. They would not break with the State Church, but form a brotherhood within it. From these small circles would grow a superior Church with broad tolerance towards people of different faith.

The Count himself studied to be a minister and permitted himself to be dedicated as a Herrnhuter 'bishop'—primarily to bring the movement's extensive foreign missions under firmer control. Then he was banished from Saxony. This, however, was an advantage for the movement, for now the Count was free to travel, inspire, and organize.

Against the Count's will the movement gradually came to be organized as a Free Church. In England its adherents were known by the name of Moravians, after the country of Moravia. Several of Wesley's friends from the Oxford period joined them.

A strongly sensuous element gradually started to creep into their preaching. The Count himself was of a strongly emotional nature. He tried, it is true, after a few years, to guide the movement along a healthier path, but his influence by that time was weakened. It was Spangenberg, whom Wesley had got to know in America, who came back and led the movement on to the course it later pursued.

But there were then few signs of decay in the Herrnhuter movement, for in 1738 Zinzendorf was at the height of his influence and was busily engaged in organizing the new estates in Herrnhut and Marienborn when Wesley set out on his pilgrimage to the land of Luther and Peter Böhler.

It was a party of five Englishmen and three Germans that set off on 14th June 1738, about three weeks after their experiences in Aldersgate Street. They landed in Holland and Wesley was very impressed by that clean and well-kept land. His adventures en route show that in those days travelling was troublesome. Often they would arrive at places where no inn would receive them, and in other places they would have to wait for hours outside the city gates while the watchmen ran off to ask the burgomaster if the strangers could be allowed in. Everywhere Wesley sought out men of faith who might strengthen him in his belief in 'the old way' to God.

In Cologne he paid a visit to the venerable old cathedral, but he was not in the least impressed, calling it 'a huge mis-shapen thing'. On the whole there was not much in Germany that aroused his enthusiasm. He enjoyed a pleasant break in Frankfurt, where he was able to go and visit Peter Böhler's father.

The first objective of Wesley's journey was the colony of Marienborn in the vicinity of Frankfurt, where there were about ninety people of various nationalities gathered together in a large building that the Count had rented. 'And here I continually met with what I sought for, viz. living proofs of the power of faith: persons saved from inward as well as outward sin by "the love of God shed abroad in their hearts", and from all doubt and fear by the abiding witness of "the Holy Ghost given unto them".'

Wesley had a number of talks with Zinzendorf and also heard him preach, but he had to go farther, right down to the borders of present-day Czechoslovakia—to Herrnhut—in order 'to see the place where the Christians live'. He travelled via Erfurt, Weimar, and Jena to Halle, where he saw the Children's Home founded by August Hermann Francke. Wesley was filled with admiration for this proof of the power of faith in the practical sphere. In the course of time he was to be responsible for the establishment of such a Home himself.

On 1st August 1738 Wesley reached Herrnhut, the colony that Zinzendorf had founded for Lutheran refugees. It comprised about a hundred houses in beautiful surroundings. The Count's own house was just a plain little building like all the rest. The travellers were given a friendly reception and provided with accommodation in the colony's guest-house. Wesley spent his time studying the discipline and organization of the Brethren. He took part in divine service and love-feasts, attended their feet-washings and studied their social work. Most important of all for him were personal talks he had with the leaders whom he asked to write down their life's experiences, so that he would always have a number of corroborations of the fact that the path he had now decided upon was the right one. The most important person for Wesley in this respect was Christian David, a former Roman Catholic who had travelled round Moravia preaching the gospel until he had been expelled. He was both minister and carpenter and had built with his own hands most of the houses in the colony. Wesley often heard him preach and made shorthand extracts of what he said.

There is no doubt that Wesley learnt a great deal on this journey to Germany. He had the same ability as Zinzendorf of being able to grasp the essentials of a matter and appropriate the best of them for himself. He did not contemplate becoming a Herrnhuter, because he found this form of Christianity too unstable and too saturated with emotion.

After staying twelve days in the colony he started on the homeward journey. This time he met Professor Francke, the son of the great pietist leader, in Halle. Relations were not good between the pietists in Halle and the United Brethren. It is therefore probable that this discussion opened Wesley's eyes to the weaker aspects of the movement to which he owed so much.

Nevertheless, the good side of life among the Brethren had impressed Wesley deeply. 'I would gladly have spent my life here; but my Master calling me to labour in another part of His vineyard, on Monday the 14th I was constrained to take my leave of this happy place; Martin Dober and a few others of the brethren walking with us about an hour. Oh when shall THIS Christianity cover the earth, as the "waters cover the sea?" '

Chapter XI

England before the Methodist Revival

SOME ACCOUNT of the England of the eighteenth century will now be needed to describe the background to Wesley's work and the needs of the age to which he brought his message.

What fills a modern reader with the greatest surprise in the study of the Church history of the day is the intimate connexion between religious issues and internal and external politics. This connexion is clear in Reformation times when the religious movement, fostered on the Continent by the prophetic ardour of Luther and Calvin, showed itself in England as Henry VIII's *coup d'état* which made him the Head of the Church in England instead of the Pope. Theological controversies were thereafter responsible for the formation not only of religious sects but also of political and social groupings. The Puritans, whose convictions demanded a non-episcopal constitution, simple ways of worship, and plain churches, were drawn on the whole from the new class of town-dwellers, some of them diligent, capable, and enterprising manufacturers and business men. They could not support the Established Church and their loyalty to the monarchy was also called into question. A series of severe laws for their suppression bore hardly on these Dissenters who became culturally, socially, and legally rootless in their own land.

Thus political controversy and religious schism weakened the life of the Church and it was further emasculated by heresies within.

Strangely enough, it was a convinced Christian, the philosopher John Locke, who was to give support to popular deistic thought. His aim was to prove that Christian doctrine was not incompatible with reason. Another thinker had previously set himself the same aim. He wanted to prove that Christianity was not mystical, but that all that Christianity taught was acceptable to reason. But here, as so often elsewhere, it happened that he who would defend Christianity before the judgement seat of reason, came instead to empty it of all real content and inward warmth, and much against his will to put a weapon in the hands of its opponents.

In 1730 appeared Matthew Tindal's book *Christianity as Old as the Creation*, a treatise that has been called the Deists' Bible. It was Tindal's intention to expound a pure religion that was a complete and stable system free from all the monstrosities that had become attached to historical and revealed religion. Christianity was superfluous, and only represented a conglomerate of suspicion and self-importance.

This form of free-thinking had crept far even into the ranks of the clergy. Another section of the clergy was busily engaged in combating deism. It mostly took the form of pamphleteering, but important theological works also first saw the light of day in this struggle.

Law's book, *A Serious Call to a Devout and Holy Life*, came into being as a protest against the Deists and their flattened, rationalistic opponents. This book, as related earlier, was to be of great importance for Wesley's future development.

Another great spirit who emerged in this conflict was the Bishop of Bristol, Joseph Butler, a fine thinker of Pascal's type. Later on, Wesley engaged in personal controversy with him.

A deist was asked why he sent his servants to church while all the time he didn't believe in the Church's message. He answered: 'So that they will not rob or murder me.' Christianity had sunk to being exclusively a guardian of morality, a first line of the police. The larger part of the clergy were occupied with the struggle against deism, but the great body of the people stood completely outside this conflict that they were in no way equipped to understand.

'Archbishops in the eighteenth century were potentates if not princes. A carriage with six horses and a private state barge on the Thames with livery-clad crew were the normal appurtenances of such a dignity,' Rowden says. 'Even Bishop Overton, who could see nothing but "stupidity and fanatical madness" in the English revival, used to ride from his castle to his cathedral—a journey of more than a hundred miles—in his episcopal carriage with his servants in livery, and when he was travelling he liked to take twelve servants with him.'

The Bishop of Winchester was in the habit of using profane language, but he used to excuse himself by saying that he swore in the company of baronets, not in the company of bishops.

Episcopal office was shared out among those who had good connexions with the court or at least with Parliament, without reference to whether the person in question was qualified for the post. A minister with a growing family would if he were circumspect, keep on good terms with those who possessed power, and we have seen that Samuel Wesley dedicated to them his poetical works.

There were, however, exceptions among these unworthy leaders of the Church; there were pious and learned men like Berkeley and Butler. But they mixed solely with their own class and had little or no connexion with the people themselves. They scarcely realized, for instance, that the Industrial Revolution had driven people in crowds to the towns and there created a proletariat—leaving behind them a partly barbaric countryside.

Nevertheless, the writer Thackeray described the situation thus after he had first sketched a grotesque picture of the corrupt life at the court of George II:

'No wonder that the clergy were corrupt and indifferent amidst this indifference and corruption. No wonder that sceptics multiplied and morals degenerated, so far as they depended on the influence of such a king. No wonder that Whitefield cried out in the wilderness, that Wesley quitted the insulted temple to pray on the hill-side. I look with reverence on those men at that time. Which is the sublimer spectacle—the good John Wesley, surrounded by his congregation of miners at the pit's mouth, or the Queen's chaplains mumbling through their morning office in their ante-room, under the picture of the great Venus, with the door opened into the adjoining chamber, where the Queen is dressing, talking scandals to Lord Hervey, or uttering sneers at Lady Suffolk.'

The economic condition of the Church gradually improved when the younger sons of the nobility began to seek honour, wealth, and power in ecclesiastical office. Obviously this, too, was of no advantage to Church life.

The Church suffered from yet another abuse called 'pluralities'. This was the system whereby a single clergyman could hold several livings at the same time. Certain members of the clergy never appeared at all in some of their parishes, though they were careful to collect their dues. They appointed a stipendiary curate on a starvation wage and let him look after the work as best he could. Even some of the bishops were equally neglectful of their work, and many of the clergy were as short of learning as of piety.

What was it like in the camp of the Dissenters? Conditions were not very much better there. Quarrels among themselves and the incessant struggle against the national Church had made their sermons polemical and arid. Furthermore, large sections of Dissent tended towards Unitarianism, that is, they did not believe in the Trinity. They regarded Jesus as a sort of ideal man and no true God. From the pulpits of the Dissenters too went forth sermons on natural religion; everything that was distinctively Christian was separated off and universal religion set in its place by many ministers, although among the exceptions could be found such a man as Isaac Watts, the great hymn-writer. Those who were wholeheartedly committed to the worship and service of God were dubbed 'enthusiasts', then a derogatory term which implied fanaticism. This term was offensive to Wesley whose intellectual clarity was never swamped by unregulated emotionalism.

It can be seen that a Christian awakening could not be expected to come from the Dissenters, as they were then. Both John Wesley's parents had deserted Dissent and returned to the State Church as the lesser evil.

We have mentioned earlier the religious societies that the German Hornech had introduced into England. Many of them belonged to the Moravian Brethren, but the majority counted themselves as members of the State Church. It was from such a group that the great evangelical awakening broke out as a life-giving stream over England's thirsting fields.

Nothing indicated that such a movement was on the threshold. The French thinker Voltaire was in England from 1726 to 1729 and he was able to pronounce: 'They have such an aversion to that sort of thing in England, that a new religion or the revival of an old could hardly reveal itself.' And old Bishop Burnet could sigh: 'I am now in my seventieth year of life, and as I cannot anyhow speak for long in this world, I cannot hope for a more golden opportunity than this, to speak out with all possible freedom. I cannot look upon it without the deepest sorrow when I see the approaching ruin that threatens this Church.'

Only a small percentage of the people could read, and writing was a luxury even for a lord. Superstition flourished. Two hundred years after the Reformation, children still learnt to pray to the saints and fortune-tellers still had a large public. Belief in ghosts and evil spirits was general.

When popular education stood at such a low level, it is obvious that this would necessarily be reflected in the pattern of popular amusement. It was unspeakably coarse. Particularly popular were the hangings at Tyburn Jail, then sought after as free entertainment. In addition one could see cock-fights, fights between bulls and dogs, or a cat tied fast to the neck of a bull, or fireworks fastened over the whole body of a bull and set alight.

The youth of the time used to go about in crowds and attack peaceful passers-by, preferably women, throw them into holes, or put them in barrels and roll them down a hill. To break a nose, knock out a few teeth or an eye, was not uncommon. It was also a common practice to give people a 'sweat-cure'. This consisted of a number of young people standing round the victim with drawn swords, pricking him so that he was kept continually in motion. It might be an act of revenge or simply 'pure' pleasure. Thirty cases of assault were reported in London in one month alone.

Gambling was also popular. The politician, Charles James Fox, in one evening alone lost two thousand pounds playing cards, and before he was twenty-four had incurred gambling debts amounting to five hundred thousand pounds. Obviously only very few could play for such sums, but even so it would not be wrong to call gambling a national disease.

It is clear that such crude pleasures could only flourish upon liberal recourse to alcohol. In 1684 gin was introduced into England. The historian Lecky says that this was a far more important event for the land than any political or military occurrence. Half a century later England was drinking half a million gallons a year. Every sixth house in London sold spirits. Many had signs outside bearing the following enticing text: 'Drunk for 1*d.*, dead drunk for 2*d.*, straw for nothing.' The dead drunk were carried down into the cellar to sleep it off, or they tottered out into the streets and slept there. Women with small children drank as heavily as the men.

In liquor's wake followed an ever greater licence in the sexual sphere. The court itself took the lead in this development. To be sure, the Queen herself did not share personally in the excesses, but she encouraged the King to be unfaithful to her and later laughed about it. The frivolous tone spread to the upper classes, where it soon became customary to speak openly of the night's debauchery, even when women were present. The theatres, too, presented plays that were immoral.

Nor was respect for human life very great. A hundred and sixty different types of crime were punishable by death, and many were the victims of these inhuman laws. A married woman who had nothing to live on because her husband had been forced into the Navy by a press-gang, went into a shop and took a piece of cloth, but put it back again when she saw she had been discovered. She was condemned to death and hanged—with her child at her breast. To steal a shilling's worth of goods from a private person, to take five shilling's worth of goods from a shop, to send a threatening letter or to saw down a tree unlawfully—all this was atoned for on the gallows.

Some there were who saw that the nation might be saved from its moral landslide. At the close of the seventeenth century, a society was formed for the reformation of morals. This society had houses of ill-fame in London closed down wholesale and was responsible for bringing a number of law-breakers to be called to account. Gamblers, drunkards, offenders against the Sabbath and swearers were either fined or imprisoned or flogged by the public executioner. In this way a number of obvious abuses were brought under control. But the power to introduce real change and a raising of moral standards such a society obviously did not possess, however well-meant its abortive efforts might have been.

For that a power from within and from above was required. A fundamental Christian revival had become a clamant need.

Chapter XII

The Doors Open

WESLEY RETURNED from his journey to Germany in September 1738, burning with eagerness to serve God. He had received ample evidence of the fact that what he had experienced in Aldersgate Street was not any isolated phenomenon.

At home in England crowds of people were perishing in sin and social injustice, while the Church was cold and almost dead. The gospel of love did not sound bright from the old pulpits. People were fobbed off with dry tracts that went far over their heads and had not the least chance of reaching the heart.

How could Wesley remedy this? As he drew near London on this foggy autumn day, he scarcely had any ideas about it. He had no dreams about becoming a Church reformer or Church leader. He wished to bear witness to the good news of God's grace, to bring the warmth of Christianity into the stiff and cold religiosity of the day. But as so often happens, he who had sworn allegiance to Christ was led by his intelligence in a direction he did not wish to go.

The orthodox minister of the Established Church—the child of many generations of ministers—was destined to come into opposition with the large majority of the English clergy. He who set his loyalty to the Church so high, was to become the originator of one of the mightiest Free Church movements of the age. The Oxford don was to send out multitudes of unacademic and unordained preachers into the towns and villages of England.

There were many such paradoxes in Wesley's life, as there probably must be in the life of anyone who is obedient to God's long-term plan, but who, at the same time, is conscious of the needs of the moment. Wesley seldom formulated plans for a long period all at once. He was, in the best sense of the word, an opportunist—he utilized opportunities as and when he had them. But all the same he never permitted his work to bear the stamp of accident. In this rare combination of opportunism and clear intention lies something of the secret of Wesley's mastery as a leader.

The young minister who returned from Germany on this September day, had no ambitious plans for the evangelization of his mother country at his feet. He simply turned to immediate tasks, answering each claim as it arose. It was natural for him to seek a connexion with the society in Fetter Lane. It was among the Christians here that he had undergone his great Christian experience. Here he had found Christian companionship and an outlet for his preaching urge and his talent for organization. The people who were accustomed to gather in these societies were mostly worthy and honest church folk. But after the Aldersgate experience Wesley's eyes were opened wider than ever, to a whole new layer of society—'the multitude that knows not the law'. They were those who had never set foot in a church, still less become accustomed to meet in a relatively exclusive religious society.

How then was he to reach these masses? The Church itself helped him in this, in that it gradually refused him the use of pulpits. After his return from Germany, the churches that opened their doors to him are dismissed usually with the following remark: 'I am to preach here no more', or 'I was informed I was not to preach any more in either of those churches'.

What was it that caused the clergy to close their doors to their zealous colleague? It was his unprecedentedly vigorous emphasis on the doctrine of justification by faith alone, a doctrine which sounded heretical to the ears of English church folk. Wesley preached it with all the fervour and pious one-sidedness of the new convert, a one-sidedness that was also made necessary by the situation. People simply did not hold the view that God saves by faith alone, still less had they had experience of it. Hence he had to preach it with all the more plainness and clarity. He deviated in no respect from the fundamental doctrines of the Church but 'from that part of the clergy who dissent from the Church'. He acknowledged himself then and later an obedient son of the true Church, the Church of England, and defended himself from every accusation of heterodoxy or dissent.

What he preached was, in reality, the old way to salvation by faith alone—that to which Jesus invited mankind, and that which Paul emphasized so strongly in his letters—this great jewel of Christianity. To be sure through the ages this doctrine had been overlaid by belief in salvation by works until finally the men of the Reformation held it up to the light in all its paradoxical simplicity and perilous freedom. God justifies the unrighteous who believe, without any further co-operation from man than the acceptance in faith of God's gift.

Once, during a morning service, Wesley had preached on this theme, but did not think he had said all he had to say about it, so he announced at the end of the sermon that he intended to continue the exposition during evensong. But this was not to be. Up sprang the parish priest and declared that there would not be any evensong with Wesley as preacher. Whereupon Wesley drew the practical conclusion: 'A good remembrance that I should, if possible, declare at *every* time the *whole* counsel of God.'

If the churches, however, were closed to him, he still had many other opportunities to preach God's word—in prison, for example. In November 1738 we find him on the scaffold itself, preparing a criminal for death. A few moments before the criminal was about to die, Wesley asked him: 'How do you feel your heart now?'

Wesley had been encouraging him with a message about instantaneous conversion and salvation through faith alone, and the condemned man answered: 'I feel a peace which I could not have believed to be possible. And I know it is the peace of God, which passeth all understanding.' Charles Wesley, who was with John on this occasion, delivered a short address to the crowd. As a general rule, Charles and George Whitefield, who had returned from one of his many tours in America, also experienced that the pulpits of the churches were closed to them.

In Fetter Lane, John Wesley experienced what Whitefield called a Pentecost season indeed. It was on 1st January 1739, when the brothers Wesley, Whitefield, Ingham, Hall, and more than sixty others were assembled at a love-feast. The great revival year 1739 was consecrated with prayer and a special experience of the power of the Spirit.

'About three in the morning, as we were continuing instant in prayer, the power of God came mightily upon us, insomuch that many cried out for exceeding joy, and many fell to the ground. As soon as we were recovered a little from that awe and amazement at the presence of His majesty we broke out with one voice, "We praise Thee, O God; we acknowledge Thee to be the Lord".'

Such experiences of God's power always filled Wesley with sacred admiration and inward joy. He never sought them for their own sake alone—to exploit them or to convert them into some form of advertisement, but he recognized them as proof of God's special presence.

He was overwhelmingly conscious of a burning call to preach the gospel of salvation, most of all to those who seemed impossible to reach, the host of the weary and heavy laden who were as sheep without a shepherd.

The human instrument God employed to lead Wesley along new paths was George Whitefield.

Born at the Bell Inn, Gloucester, on 16th December 1714, he was eleven years younger than John Wesley. His grandfather had been a clergyman but his father had an inn which his mother kept up after she was widowed at a relatively early age. George was then only two years old, and grew up here in the tavern, working as a tapster from his fifteenth to his seventeenth year.

Then he was invited to become a servitor at Oxford University. In return for his services to the wealthier students, he received free board and study. Here he came into contact with the Wesley brothers and became a zealous member of the Holy Club. He delivered his first sermon after his ordination in 1736 and soon showed himself to be a very talented public speaker. At twenty-two he already had the reputation of being one of the country's most engrossing preachers.

Modesty was never his strongest trait. At twenty-five he published a book of seventy-six pages entitled: *A Short Account of God's dealings with the Reverend Mr George Whitefield, A.B., late of Pembroke-College, Oxford, from his Infancy to the Time of his entering into Holy Orders.*

With the fervour of the new convert he described his old life as immoderately sinful. Comparatively innocent boyish pranks were regarded as a sign of boundless depravity. Even in his childhood years his histrionic ability was apparent. He appeared in children's plays and displayed great dramatic power. In addition he described his 'conversion', his fall, his victory, and escape from the grip of temptation.

This sincere depiction of a young man's difficulties aroused horror in ecclesiastical circles. The Bishop of Exeter, Dr Lavington, wrote thus: 'Mr Whitefield's account of God's dealings with him is such a boyish, ludicrous, filthy, nasty, and shameless relation of himself, as quite defiles paper, and is shocking to decency and modesty.'

The Bishop certainly painted an overcoloured picture, but there was truth behind his exaggerated statement. Whitefield appeared at times to be guilty of pride about his achievement, particularly about the surprising advances that he, the former tapster, made amongst the nobility.

Certain letters he sent to Wesley during a later controversy can only be characterized as stupid. Whitefield was not a scholar and had not acquired exact methods of study; he himself did not realize his limitations, but he was destined to be less influential than Wesley. He had a lively and glancing mind and a melodious delivery and with the fire of his nature and his buoyant eloquence he captivated the large gatherings that streamed to hear him. 'His lips dropped like the honeycomb and were a well of life', as Lady Huntingdon somewhat extravagantly said of him.

Sir James Stephen gives a fairly acute characterization: 'The lessons which he never drew from books were never taught him by living men. He allowed himself no leisure for social intercourse with his superiors, or with his equals, but underwent the debilitating effects of conversing, almost exclusively, with those who sat as disciples at his feet. Their homage, and the impetuous tumult of his career, left him but superficially acquainted with himself. Unsuspicious of his own ignorance, and exposed to flattery far more intoxicating than the acclamations of the theatre, he laid the foundations of a new religious system with less of profound thought, and in a greater penury of theological research, than had ever fallen to the lot of a reformer or heresiarch before.'

But this is far from the whole truth about Whitefield. No one can call him devoid of a serious and sincere Christianity. His success as an evangelist was fundamentally due to the love he felt for the destitute.

The same writer, Stephen, also says of him: 'If ever philanthropy burned in the human heart with a pure and intense flame, embracing the whole family of man in the spirit of universal charity, it was in the heart of George Whitefield. . . . "He loved the world that hated him." He had no preferences but in favour of the ignorant, the miserable, and the poor.'

He could carry an audience to the heights or reduce them to tears. Samuel Johnson, said of him: 'He would be followed by crowds were he to wear a nightcap in the pulpit.'

The historian, Green, certainly sums up the nature of Whitefield's preaching when he speaks of 'its intense reality, its earnestness of belief and its deep tremulous sympathy with the sin and sorrow of mankind'.

When he travelled to Bristol to collect money for his mission work and his orphanage in Georgia, he experienced the same fate as in London: the churches were gradually closed to him. He heard mocking remarks like: 'If Whitefield is so interested in converting the heathen, why doesn't he go to Kingswood?'

Kingswood was a little mining village near Bristol whose people were said to be scarcely civilized. They possessed no church and no minister and no one took any interest in them at all. Whitefield took the scornful remark as a sign from God. One day a rumour passed through Kingswood that Whitefield had come to the place, and quickly a crowd of some two hundred miners assembled. He preached to them standing on rising ground on 17th February 1739, an important date in the history of the Methodist revival.

As things went so well on the first occasion, he tried once again. This time about two thousand people were assembled, and the crowd increased steadily, until it was estimated that some twenty thousand people were present at Whitefield's open-air meeting. Even if we accept the figure with reservation, and even if we, like one Methodist historian, Curnock, divide the largest figures by ten, it is nevertheless a fact that open-air meetings were very popular and filled a mighty need of the time.

It was a moving sight to see the great crowds of people who assembled about the preacher and listened spellbound to the glad message. To think that someone cared about them! The tears ran down their black cheeks and left white stripes in the grime! Many were converted at these meetings, and Whitefield went on preaching in the open air in Bristol itself, also with a happy outcome. Crowds streamed to the meetings in numbers no one had ever dared to hope.

Many other tasks also made their claim on Whitefield. He had to return to Georgia and there were many friends to visit first, so he wrote to Wesley and asked him to come to Bristol and take over the great work there.

Wesley was at first very dubious and made many objections: 'I could scarce reconcile myself at first to this strange way of preaching in the fields . . . having been all my life (till very lately) so tenacious of every point relating to decency and order, that I should have thought the saving of souls almost a sin if it had not been done in a church.'

After clear guidance from God, however, he agreed to make the journey, even if the passages of Scripture he read on the journey were very gloomy and seemed to forebode an early death. Charles viewed it all with disfavour.

On 2nd April 1739, John preached before about three thousand people on a common outside Bristol. The *Cambridge Modern History* attaches the highest significance to this event: 'While Whitefield was sailing to Georgia, John Wesley "proclaimed in the highways the glad tidings of salvation, speaking from a little eminence in a ground adjoining to the city (Bristol), to about three thousand people". From this day, April 2 1739, may be reckoned a new era in the religious history of England; for her greatest religious leader between Cromwell and Newman had found his way to the hearts of her people.'

Wesley had taken over Whitefield's work. It was to prove a happy release. For even though the latter could take the masses by storm, it was proved in London for instance, where he preached at a number of open-air meetings a few weeks later, that what he did was seldom of lasting value, whereas Wesley's preaching seems to have had a deep and more durable influence.

Wesley was undoubtedly an organizer of considerable ability. He never struck a blow without first knowing that he would be able to follow up the victory; the flock, once gathered, must be shepherded. He worked untiringly as a pastor so that the fruits of the revival might be preserved. A later entry in his *Journal* expresses this principle. 'We stopped an hour in Mullingar. The sovereign [i.e. the Governor] of the town came to the inn, and expressed much desire that I should preach. But I had little hopes of doing good by preaching in a place where I could preach but once.'

Every prospective Methodist minister must still study an appointed selection of Wesley's sermons before he is accepted into the ministry. Many readers have wondered how these sermons could have made such a powerful impression on the crowds. They have probably acquired a somewhat more literary character than his sermons had when they were preached, but they have not been materially altered either in form or content, otherwise there would have been protests from many who had heard them first delivered.

For his open-air meetings, Wesley used only a limited number of texts, all of a central nature and easily understood, and he delivered his message with quiet conviction and secret joy. If the mob made a noise at the start, he would usually finish off quickly. Usually they were so gripped by what they heard, that they drank in every word.

Wesley's sermons presumed a certain knowledge of the Scriptures —something that people in those days possessed in far greater measure than the restless children of today. They give a brilliant introduction to the thought of the Scriptures and preserve a delicate balance between law and gospel. Wesley was no Apollo as an orator. He is more like Paul, though without the numerous intercalated subordinate clauses that characterize this great apostle and help to make his letters 'hard to be understood'. To a greater degree than appears general in the preaching of our own day. Wesley drew his thoughts about Christianity from the apostle John. He also gave prominence to this apostle as a model for young preachers in matters of choice of word and style.

We have to accept that the ultimate reason for Wesley's great progress as a preacher lay in his heart-warming simplicity. He spoke so simply that all ordinary people were able to follow him and he avoided like the plague all difficult words and technical philosophical phrases. It was for this reason that the fruits were so enduring and his influence so powerful.

Particularly in the early period Wesley's preaching caused many reactions of shouting, terror, despair, and jubiliation. People fell to the ground as though dead and rose to their feet again with souls filled with joy. They might at any moment suddenly pass from blackest despair to heaven-storming gladness. It is worth noting that there were far more instances of ecstasy under the sober preaching of John Wesley than under the dramatic rhetoric of George Whitefield.

A weaver named John Haydon had been a witness to the fact that a Quaker had been transported with joy during one of Wesley's meetings. He himself was a very precise High Churchman, and he now attended often in order to prove to his own circle that what had happened at Wesley's meetings was an evil and empty mockery. But one day as he was sitting down to eat his lunch he started to read a sermon he had borrowed. It was Wesley's sermon 'Salvation by Faith'. When he reached the last page, he turned as pale as a corpse, shouted aloud, and fell off his chair on to the floor.

This attracted the attention of his neighbours and a whole crowd of people assembled outside the house where he lived. Wesley was sent for and found the house was filled with people when he arrived in the middle of the night. At first the wife would not let him in, but Haydon himself shouted: 'No, let them all come; let all the world see the just judgement of God.' When Wesley entered, he was lying on the floor with several men holding him down. When he caught sight of Wesley, he pointed to him and shouted: 'Aye, this is he who I said was a deceiver of the people; but God has overtaken me. I said it was all a delusion; but this is no delusion. . . . O thou devil! thou cursed devil! Yea, thou legion of devils! Thou canst not stay. Christ will cast thee out. I know His work is begun. Tear me to pieces, if thou wilt; but thou canst not hurt me.'

Wesley and his friends prayed for him and the man was freed in both body and soul. When Wesley visited him next day, he was filled with a transfigured peace and joy.

In the great movement that arose around Wesley, there were doubtless many people of unsound mind impelled by an insatiable urge to assert themselves, and they were very harmful to the movement. Consequently Wesley frequently announced that he did not think any more highly of a person merely because he interrupted him, and this usually ensured peace.

Wesley's *Journal* at this time is a rich field for people wishing to study the labyrinths of the human mind. Charles Wesley says of this period: 'Many, no doubt, were, at our first preaching, struck down, both soul and body, into the depth of distress. Their *outward affections* were easy to be imitated.'

Cases of ecstasy, however, were not nearly so frequent as a later age seemed to believe, and they were in not any way typical of the evangelical revival.

It is of interest to note how the three great Methodist leaders reacted to the vociferous outbreaks at the meetings. It tells us not a little about themselves.

Charles Wesley brushed them aside without more ado. At one of his meetings there were some women who were moaning and wailing and trying to stay near the preacher. He had them shown into a corner. This proved to be effective, for afterwards not a sound escaped them.

Whitefield experienced almost nothing of this sort of thing. He writes to Wesley in an almost fatherly tone, exhorting him to check disturbances, but one has the feeling while reading him that Whitefield felt a little put out that his own preaching did not have a corresponding effect.

John Wesley even went so far as to regard many of these outbreaks as the machinations of the devil sent to hinder him in his work, but he realized, too, that this could not be the whole explanation. Consequently, he made a point of visiting those who had behaved in an unusual manner at the meetings, questioned them closely and systematically about what they had felt and experienced, and then conscientiously recorded it. Many of these accounts he later had printed in his *Journal* without further comment. There they stand for what they are worth.

Wesley often says about himself that he 'called out' or 'cried aloud' to the Lord, and in this he was not far removed from that exuberance which in his simpler followers found spontaneous and direct expression. He had himself lived through a spiritual spring, with the thaws of spring and the warmth and life that followed. Like Bjørnsen he knew that spring 'makes little noise'. But as these spontaneous expressions of powerful emotion gradually became less frequent and finally ceased to occur, he did not lament the fact; he had never consciously sought to call forth or stimulate such phenomena.

Never, not even at the time when the revival was at its height, did he regard these manifestations as a particular sign of God's presence. Proof of the genuineness of the preaching and conversion was for Wesley always of a moral character. Was faith active in good deeds? Had God's love been poured out in the lives of believers in such a way that their conduct bore the stamp of it?

John's eldest brother, Samuel, the teacher, was much disturbed about what he heard of his younger brother's work. He wrote advising him strongly against the great spectre of this rationalistic age, 'enthusiasm', imagination, and fantasy. Wesley defended the revival zealously and with real earnestness against these charges. The proof of the genuineness of the revival was, he wrote to his brother, that drinkers were reformed, harlots cleansed, Sabbath-breakers and swearers saved, and that all these were led into a new way of life.

In London it was again Whitefield who got Wesley to speak in the open-air. He did it with great success, but here, too, with doubts at the start.

During this year Wesley travelled several times back and forth between the centres of the Methodist revival, Bristol and London. Crowds of people came to God, and there was much for him to do. Several times, too, he was invited to visit his beloved Oxford, and when they heard that their eldest brother, Samuel, had died, John and Charles travelled together to Tiverton to console their sister-in-law. Samuel had been a man with the courage of his convictions, and his sympathies in politics lay with the Jacobite cause. For this reason he never received the recognition from his contemporaries to which he was entitled. He was an industrious writer and a good writer of verse in the style of the day. He was austerely High Church and, as stated earlier, opposed to the work of his younger brothers. However, he lived to see the labour pains of the revival, mainly through reports. It is certain that he was a conscientious Christian and Maldwyn Edwards is certainly right when he says: 'There are not two brothers to be remembered. There are three.'

When Wesley reached the house of mourning, he found that his sister-in-law 'was sorrowing almost as one without hope. Yet we could not but rejoice at hearing from one who had attended my brother in all his weakness, that, several days before he went hence, God had given him a calm and full assurance of his interest in Christ. Oh may every one who opposes it be thus convinced that this doctrine is of God!'

In what follows, we shall endeavour to follow the Methodist revival in so far as it affects Wesley's own life or is indebted to him. Henceforth his life was bound up with it, for if we exclude the Grace Murray episode and later his unhappy marriage, it can be said that the whole of his life was consecrated to the work God had given him and it can in no way be any longer regarded as a 'private life'.

Chapter XIII

The Boundaries are Drawn

THE LEADERS of the evangelical revival were united in their belief in justification by faith, but on many other doctrinal questions they did not agree, and there followed painful ruptures between old friends who placed love of truth higher than the demands of personal friendship. Frontiers were drawn that divided the followers of Wesley from the United Brethren and from other Methodists with Calvinistic views.

As we have seen, the Anglican clergy opposed Wesley's 'new' doctrines. His open-air meetings made matters worse, and true or distorted accounts of the ecstatic phenomena at the meetings increased their antagonism. Anti-Methodist literature, mostly pamphlets and fly-sheets that warned people of the moral dangers of the doctrine of justification by faith alone, condemned Wesley and his followers as fanatics and counselled people to turn a deaf ear to this new heresy.

The Church authorities were alarmed by the proportions of the movement, and Charles was summoned to appear before the Archbishop of Canterbury. He received a severe reprimand and was threatened with expulsion from the Church if he did not discontinue his new activities. Charles had been the whole of his life bound by custom and tradition in Church matters, and gave serious consideration to what had transpired in this conversation. Fortunately, Whitefield was in the neighbourhood and succeeded in brushing aside his misgivings with healthy vehemence. The result was that Charles, the very next Sunday, preached in Moorfields in London, and in this way gave the Archbishop the answer that one ought to obey God rather than man.

In Bristol, John was sent for by Bishop Joseph Butler, the lovable and learned philosopher who fought the Deists so persistently. The Bishop started the discussion with an attack on the doctrine of justification by faith alone. According to Wesley's own account he had no difficulty in driving the Bishop into a corner on that issue. However, Butler renewed the attack—using the argument of the orderliness of Church organization and the authority of the bishops. He said to Wesley in a serious tone:

'Well, sir, . . . you have no business here; you are not commissioned to preach in this diocese. Therefore I advise you to go hence.'

Then Wesley gave the quiet and dignified answer that has remained the classic expression of the affirmation of his calling:

'My lord, my business on earth is to do what good I can. Wherever, therefore, I think I can do most good there must I stay, so long as I think so. At present I think I can do most good here; therefore, here I stay. As to my preaching here, a dispensation of the gospel is committed to me, and woe is me if I preach not the gospel wherever I am in the habitable world! . . . I do not . . . conceive that in preaching here . . . I break any human law. When I am convinced I do, then it will be time to ask, "Shall I obey God or man?" '

Arnold Lunn comments on this episode thus: 'And so they parted. The Bishop went back to his books with a sigh. He was a great man, and perhaps Wesley's visit had left him vaguely uneasy. He may have found it difficult to concentrate on his beloved Deists. Who were these colliers of Kingswood to whom the arrogant young man had referred so often? . . . Were they in his diocese? . . . What parish were they in? . . . He really must look into the matter.'

In a solemn public declaration some years later, Wesley said that the Methodists were willing to obey all the Church's laws as they understood them by the light of their own conscience. With the same reservation they would also obey the bishops as the dispensers of these laws, but they would pay no heed to the personal opinions and desires of the bishops outside the laws of the Church.

That it should often be the clergy who created the greatest difficulties for Wesley can readily be understood from the political situation. The means they employed were many and various, and they were often to be found allying themselves with the mob. But Wesley's office in the Church of God was not to be shaken by such circumstances as these. His calling remained sure while his work under the guidance of God took different forms.

His connexion with the United Brethren, the Herrnhuters, brought different problems.

Although the little company in Fetter Lane found their meetings a means of grace they were far from attaining unbroken spiritual unity there. On the contrary, there were often disputes and scenes among the members. Frequently these had their origin in purely personal antagonisms, but on other occasions differences of opinion about basic tenets of belief or about their relationship to the Established Church split the fellowship. Not infrequently, unbalanced and fanatical people would force their way into the meeting and create disturbance and confusion. The meetings thus bore the stamp of those difficulties that every revivalist gathering sooner or later has to contend with.

More often than not it was Wesley who had to restore order in these disputes and as a mediator he was well-endowed. In other matters it was Charles who took charge in his more forceful manner.

In June 1739, Wesley returned to London from Bristol. The meeting had now come under the influence of a French 'prophetess' who shouted aloud every time Charles spoke. All in all she betrayed considerable interest in him, but Charles was not going to be imposed upon by the woman's 'spiritual' performance. Instead he investigated her private life and found she was living in sin, and he took immediate action.

Even worse was the fact that completely false doctrines had begun to creep in, doctrines of a type that could have the most harmful effects on Christian conduct. A German clergyman, Pastor Molther, a capable and extremely popular man, now appeared and insisted that one could not have faith unless one also had full knowledge and the immanent testimony of the Spirit. There was no such thing as weak faith, he said. Therefore, one should not employ means of grace, for that was the law's doing. One should simply remain quiet. Prayer, Communion, Bible-reading, and attendance at Church one could either take part in or ignore, just as one wished. There was only one command: thou shalt believe, and always remain calm!

Wesley reacted violently to this error, which was a caricature of salvation by faith alone. As so often happened, however, it was Charles who was more eager to do battle. John tried negotiation for as long as possible before embarking on any fateful break unless he were forced to do it in God's cause. But finding all attempts at meditation useless, he wrote on 22nd June 1740: 'Finding there was no time to delay, without utterly destroying the cause of God, I began to execute what I had long designed—to strike at the root of the grand delusion.' This took the form of a sermon on the text, 'Stand ye in the way, ask for the old paths'.

As a result of this the group in Fetter Lane decided that he could not preach there again. He was barred not only from the pulpits of the official Church, but also from the narrower brotherhood in Fetter Lane where he and so many others had received spiritual nourishment and where he himself had been able to be of help and comfort to so many.

But four weeks later Wesley was again in the gathering when a love-feast was held. At the end of the meeting he read aloud an explanation of his views on 'weak faith' and the means of grace:

'I have warned you hereof again and again, and besought you to turn back to the Law and the Testimony. I have borne with you long, hoping you would turn. But as I find you more and more confirmed in the error of your ways, nothing now remains but that I should give you up to God. You that are of the same judgement, follow me.'

Wesley was followed by eighteen or nineteen others who together formed the first Methodist society. They started to hold their meetings in an abandoned cannon foundery, where Wesley had already preached God's Word at an earlier date.

Böhler, Spangenborg, and Count Zinzendorf himself tried to bring about a reconciliation, but in vain. The breach was an accomplished fact.

Later events proved that Wesley's decision was right. By 1743 they had 1,950 members, while the United Brethren had seventy-two. This fact did not prevent Zinzendorf from inserting an announcement in a newspaper, where he made it clear that he had nothing to do with the Wesley brothers. He added that these two would soon be running their heads against a wall!

Zinzendorf was now gaining more influence over the United Brethren in England and not for the good of the movement. In the heat of the strife we find Wesley—in the manner of the age—using harsh words about his old friends 'the German wolves', who taught freedom from all laws. But this did not prevent him, nevertheless, from giving his old friends the following true testimonial: 'Next to these [i.e. "some thousands in our own Church who have the faith and love which is among them, without those errors either of judgement or practice"], the body of the Moravian Church, however mistaken some of them are, are in the main, of all whom I have seen, the best Christians in the world.'

Wesley wished to make it clear that it was not on doctrinal grounds that he had broken with the United Brethren. 'I would wish all to observe that the points in question between us and either the German or English Antinomians[1] are not points of opinion, but of practice. We break with no man for his opinion. We think, and let think.'

The following conversation between Wesley and one of the 'Antinomians' makes it clear how necessary it was for him to break with 'this great fallacy'. John Wesley reports a conversation he had at Birmingham with one of the pillars of their society.

'Do you believe you have nothing to do with the law of God?'

'I have not; I am not under the law: I live by faith.'

'Have you, as living by faith, a right to everything in the world?'

'I have; all is mine, since Christ is mine.'

'May you, then, take anything you will anywhere? Suppose out of a shop, without the consent or knowledge of the owner?'

'I may, if I want it; for it is mine. Only I will not give offence.'

'Have you also a right to all the women in the world?'

'Yes, if they consent.'

'And is not that a sin?'

[1] 'Antinomianism' is a general name for the view that Christians are by grace released from the need of observing any moral law.

'Yes, to him that thinks it is a sin; but not to those whose *hearts are free.*'

Uncompromising is Wesley's comment: 'Surely these are the firstborn children of Satan!'

The members of the Fetter Lane gathering had never actually belonged to the United Brethren, so that Wesley had never been a member of any Moravian organization. On the other hand it was through the Moravians that he had come to believe in salvation by faith alone, and it was among them that he had experienced his evangelical conversion. Some of them had become life-long friends. United with the Moravians in belief he deprecated their lax discipline.

He was soon to find himself in conflict with obstinate Calvinistic thought, with its teaching of double predestination, that is, that some are chosen for eternal salvation and others for eternal damnation. Wesley described the whole system in less than fifty words: 'The sum of all this is—One in twenty, suppose, of mankind is elected; nineteen in twenty are reprobated. The elect shall be saved do what they will: the reprobate shall be damned do what they can. Reader, believe this, or be damned.'

This controversial question which had long burdened Christendom was also destined to divide the Methodist revival in England into two camps: one Calvinistic, under the leadership of George Whitefield, and a far bigger 'Arminian' one under John Wesley, with his message of the grace of God, available for every man.

Whitefield during his stay in America came under the influence of clergymen who staunchly supported the Calvinistic doctrine; Jonathan Edwards, in particular, the colony's great evangelist, made an ineffaceable impression upon him. Whitefield came to regard himself as one of God's chosen people and based his hope of salvation on this belief. It is hard to see how he could be such a fervent evangelist and winner of souls and yet could think that the rejected were lost and the chosen saved whatever they did; he himself explained this by saying that one could never know who had been chosen.

John Wesley had reached his conclusions about this as early as 1725. It was then that he discussed predestination with his good counsellor in theological matters—his mother. Wesley's logical nature and the strongly rationalistic trait in his outlook rebelled against a teaching that made God appear unjust and unloving and the quest for holiness superfluous. The Calvinist Beza had said: 'We believe, though it is incomprehensible, that it is just to damn such as do not deserve it.' Wesley set against this God's universal love, His manifest and saving grace and the necessity of working out our salvation in fear and trembling.

Whitefield begged Wesley to keep this controversial question out of his preaching. Even if the leaders themselves were able to impose such reticence upon themselves, their followers could not be expected to do so. It was generally known that the leaders had different opinions on this matter, and this fact caused no little perturbation. Some of Whitefield's followers introduced the question into the Methodist society as a controversial issue, and on 29th April 1739, Wesley found it necessary to deliver his sermon 'Free Grace' in Bristol. Just after this, Charles had printed and published a hymn, in which he, too, clearly teaches that grace is for everyone. Whitefield had begged Wesley not to have his sermon printed, but when the lots were cast he received the reply: 'Preach and print!'

This sermon was sent to Whitefield, who at that time was in America. A whole correspondence on the matter developed between them. In the heat of the battle, Whitefield, the younger of the two, sent Wesley this letter:

'Dear brother Wesley,

What mean you by disputing in all your letters? May God give you to know yourself; and then you will not plead for *absolute perfection* or call the doctrine of *election* a "doctrine of devils". My dear brother, take heed. See you are in Christ a new creature. Beware of a false peace. Strive to enter in at the strait gate; and give all diligence to make your calling and election sure. Remember you are but a babe in Christ, if so much. Be humbled; talk little; think and pray much. Let God teach you; and He will lead you into all truth. I love you heartily. I pray you may be kept from error, both in principle and practice. Salute all the brethren. If you must dispute, stay till you are master of the subject; otherwise you will hurt the cause you would defend. Study to adorn the gospel of our Lord in all things; and forget not to pray for your affectionate friend and servant, George Whitefield.'

This somewhat confused letter was printed without Whitefield's permission and distributed by his friends before a meeting in the Foundery at which Wesley was to preach. When he appeared in the pulpit, he said he would do the same with the letter as he thought Whitefield would have done if he had been present. Then he tore the letter in pieces, and the whole of the congregation followed his example.

Meanwhile, Whitefield had returned home from America. He now dissociated himself publicly from the brothers Wesley, and even said that 'Mr Wesley and I preach two different gospels'. Bitter words passed on both sides, but Wesley showed greater moderation in his choice of expression.

This deep rift in Methodism interfered with its work for some time, but for all that it was better that things went as they did, 'for beyond all personal friendships and human considerations is the question of truth'.

The old trio were later reconciled, however, and their friendship restored. They spoke at each other's meetings and met privately when they were able. We have a splendid testimony of this in a letter Charles Wesley sent to his wife twenty-five years later. 'Last night my brother came. This morning we spent two blessed hours with G. Whitefield. The threefold cord, we trust, will never more be broken.'

At the hands of the genuine Calvinists Wesley later had to suffer a great deal, not least during the critical period of his marriage. The editor of the Calvinistic *Gospel Magazine*, the hymn-writer Toplady, was not above making the following startling assertions against Wesley: 'Wesley is guilty of Satanic shamelessness'; of 'acting the ignoble part of a lurking, sly assassin'; of 'uniting the sophistry of a Jesuit with the authority of a pope', 'and of sinking the discussion "to the level of an oyster woman".'

But in spite of these controversies—in which John often had to stand alone, his work continued and grew, and a time of consolidation lay ahead.

Chapter XIV

The Structure Rises

WHEN WESLEY was in Bristol in the spring of 1739, he found that three women there had already formed the habit of meeting weekly for religious fellowship, and soon afterwards four young men agreed to meet together in the same way. These were the first Methodist classes, though they did not yet bear that name.

Wesley soon realized that the Methodists would have to acquire premises for their activities, so they purchased a site. Four days later the foundation stone of the first Methodist place of worship in the world was laid, and great was the rejoicing among the members in Bristol.

Wesley had appointed a committee of twelve men to collect money for the building, but he soon found out that they were not doing anything. If the work was not to come to a standstill, he himself had to assume responsibility, and before he knew where he was, he was in debt to the extent of one hundred and fifty pounds. With no money and no apparent prospect of getting any, he confidently declared, 'But I knew "the earth is the Lord's and the fulness thereof", and in His name set out, nothing doubting.'

Wesley was the real and legal owner of the property—something which in these restless years of conflict was a real advantage. He also consolidated his work in Bristol by splitting up the membership into classes, each with its own leader and these classes soon increased in number.

Simultaneously, Wesley took over the project that Whitefield had begun, a school for the children of the miners in Kingswood. The newly-converted in Kingswood attended the churches in Bristol in such numbers that the ministers there became both anxious and irritated—irritated because on Communion Sundays they did not get home for lunch until very late in the afternoon, and anxious because they did not properly understand this half-civilized multitude from the mining village that no one previously had bothered about. The clergy considered these people did not belong to their parish and denied them the Lord's Supper—with the result that the people attached themselves still more closely to the warm-hearted and fervent evangelists who had wakened them from their sinful sleep.

Wesley, himself, now independent of other premises, began to hold meetings three times a day, and his preaching showed remarkable results: instant conversions, frequently amidst tears, attacks of fainting, and emotional outbreaks. The Methodist societies gladly welcomed the new converts and new life and gladness flowed into the drab mining district as the people's hearts were lifted to God. But the Church, cold and hostile, opposed this new life, permitting a God-sent opportunity to slip by.

But Wesley also had to find premises in London. We have mentioned how he had an old cannon foundery at his disposal. On the 11th November 1739 he had preached for the first time on the spot that had once been a king's foundery. Churchill's great ancestor, the Duke of Marlborough, had captured a large number of cannons during his campaign on the Continent and this foundery was established to recast them, later being damaged by an explosion.

It was cold holding meetings out of doors, and even a half-ruined building was welcome when Wesley bought it for one hundred and fifteen pounds. Repairs brought the cost up to about eight hundred pounds—a considerable amount, and these premises were to remain the London headquarters of Methodism right up to 1778, when the City Road Chapel was built.

The Foundery held about fifteen hundred people. In addition, there were living-rooms for Wesley, a schoolroom, and rooms for 'band meetings' and other small groups. Here too the preachers had their stable and their coach-house. The women sat in the front gallery and underneath it, while the men were accommodated in and beneath the side galleries. The twelve extra seats for women just in front of the pulpit were provided with a unique luxury—back-rests. In the little apartment Wesley had furnished for himself, Susanna Wesley passed the last years of her life and followed the growing revivalist movement with prayer and gratitude.

An eye-witness described divine service at the Foundery in June 1740. The meeting began at five o'clock in the morning and was extremely simple. The building certainly displayed no pomp or splendour and was indeed still dilapidated. The pulpit was constructed of rough planks nailed together, and broken plaster on both ceiling and walls revealed rotting beams. At five o'clock precisely Wesley emerged from his quarters and a whisper passed through the assembly: 'Here he comes!' After a hymn Wesley delivered an extempore prayer and then began to preach. The man who recorded this service was so deeply affected by Wesley's words that he vowed: 'As long as I live I will never part from him.'

More than six months before the breach with Fetter Lane, some eight or ten people had come to Wesley and asked him to guide them in spiritual matters and pray with them. They seemed to be genuinely convinced of their sinfulness and were filled with a desire to escape the approaching wrath of God. Wesley made a note of their names and addresses and undertook to visit them regularly. But gradually the number of people requiring such visits increased, and it took up too much of Wesley's time. He therefore asked them to meet together every Thursday evening, the very same evening as his mother had chosen for ministering to his soul when he was a child. He did the same in the three other Methodist centres—Bristol, Kingswood, and Bath. This is the origin of the weekly Methodist class-meeting.

The need to obtain money drove Wesley farther along the paths of organizing activity. How was the Methodist society in Bristol to pay for the house in the Horse Fair? Captain Foy suggested that each member should give one penny per week until the debt was paid. ' "But many of them", said one, "have not a penny to give." "True," said the Captain; "then put ten or twelve of them to me. Let each of these give what they can weekly, and I will supply what is wanting." Many others made the same offer.' This marked yet another stage in the building up of the Methodism class system.

Wesley soon realized that here he had a God-given tool for the care of souls and the maintenance of Church discipline. He could not visit all the members himself, but now through the class-leaders he was able to keep in touch with the very large number of people who had been converted. Some needed admonishment or reproof, others whose way of life was harmful to the cause had to be expelled, but the great majority of the converts gained inspiration and uplift from the class-leaders' visits.

It was not always convenient, however, to hold spiritual conversation in the homes or places of employment of the Methodists, so it was agreed that they should meet the class-leaders in somebody's home, or in some other place where they knew they were welcome. In this way the class-meetings became the focal points of expanding Methodism. It was the class-leaders who gave timely rebuke, instruction, and encouragement. The members confessed to one another their sins and their discoveries, prayed together and cheered one another, and came with their offerings for the support of the preachers. Collections were seldom taken at Wesley's public services.

Naturally there were many who felt no love for this new form of Christian activity, particularly as many of the class-leaders were unfitted for their work. But the fact remains that the work was growing and that this new régime, brought about by a combination of circumstances, was a means of confirming the converts in the faith and allowing Wesley to extend the work northwards and later throughout the country.

The ideals from the Holy Club and Oxford Methodism had in no way lost their grip on Wesley. For this reason he also wanted to have his 'bands' and 'select societies', and to these chosen groups there came those who were pressing on towards perfection in holiness. These 'bands' disappeared gradually despite his persistent attempts to keep them alive, but the class system has been retained in Methodism until the present day. Class tickets, renewed once a quarter, served as useful proof of good conduct. For all the pastoral care of the class-leaders Wesley did not become any less diligent in his visiting. The *Journal* contains examples of how he devoted whole weeks to this work alone. He would often go out at six in the morning and keep it up until six in the evening. History does not record what the housewives thought when they received visits at six o'clock in the morning!

In his shaping of the class system Wesley did not depend on Scriptural endorsement; it was enough for him that it was effective in caring for the newly-converted and helping the more mature along the path of sanctification. A formal resemblance to some of early Christianity's institutions meant little to him. Again, he would gladly have let the whole of his system go if he could have found anything better but nothing better emerged, and it was in these small groups that the Christians learnt to 'submit themselves to one another in the fear of God'. Wesley was never a slave to the letter of the word, no dry pedant, no rider of a hobby horse. He was a pragmatist, using all that came his way to serve the work of the Gospel. Few of his achievements were entirely original. 'He no more invented this than the architect invented the brick.' But how he used it! And how he shaped the bricks!

From among the institutions of primitive Christianity he revived the love-feast—the agape—where the believers assembled to pray and to share their spiritual experiences. In addition he revived the vigils of the early Church in which the believers spent the whole of the night in prayer to God. Incidentally, it was a newly-converted miner from Kingswood who suggested it. Having formerly spent his Saturday nights in dissipation and drink, he now wanted to spend that same time in God's house. Wesley agreed, and watch-night services were held on one Saturday evening and night each month, and later once a quarter. Now it is celebrated only on New Year's Eve. We have seen that Wesley never struck a blow without reasonable hope of being able to follow it up and to speak only once at a place seemed to him of little value. When he had finished speaking he used to explain to his congregation what Methodism was and invited those interested to remain behind and form a Methodist society. In this way such societies sprang up all over the land from the time when Wesley set out on his unending journey round the towns and villages of this land in 1742.

The 'Covenant Services' which Wesley arranged, although making use of Puritan devotional writings were mainly Methodist in origin and were founded with the idea that believers ought regularly to renew their covenant with God.

Wesley loved his life in London and the London Methodists loved him, but his ministry was not to begin and end there. The country lay open before him. First and foremost he was attracted by the North—to Newcastle, to the Lincolnshire of his childhood, and above all to his beloved Epworth!

Chapter XV

The Way North

WHEN JOHN and Charles Wesley returned from America they expected to come back to a life of academic ease. Charles was advised to become a teacher in a school, and John to resume his position at the University. Instead they were thrown out into a sphere of ever-expanding work, and peace and quiet were no more to be found. Almost without respite the two brothers found themselves involved in something radically new to their age, the life of an itinerant preacher. It was not the first time in the history of England that men had travelled around preaching the Word of God. The old Saxon bishops had done it, so had various Catholic monastic orders, and at one time the Quakers also. But this was at least seventy years before, and the generation that witnessed John and Charles Wesley travelling on horseback through England was both amazed and confused—often, too, annoyed.

There were among the converts many young men with a burning warmth of heart, a living and personal experience of God's grace, a good example of Christian conduct, and many even with an inner longing to speak of their Saviour and to preach God's Word. The first instance of Methodist lay preaching is said to have occurred in 1739. Whitefield had been giving an address in a churchyard, and when he had finished, a certain Mr Bowers stepped forward to speak to the people. In vain Charles Wesley tried to stop him and left the churchyard in protest with some of his friends. Bowers admitted later that he might have done wrong, but that he had thought that it was the Spirit of God who had inspired him to speak. He was seriously reprimanded by Wesley some time later when he was preaching God's Word in the streets of Oxford; put in irons by the authorities he was only released when he solemnly promised Wesley that he would never again do such a thing.

Wesley had hoped that the clergy would interest themselves in the new converts, but in vain. He often found that when he returned to places where he had worked, many of the new converts had gone back to their old way of life. Sometimes he succeeded in reclaiming the strayed, but more often he did not. Then he appointed some of their own circle to look after them while he himself was away. They had to be God-fearing men with sound judgement and a living urge to meet the faithful for mutual edification. He therefore appointed Thomas Maxfield in London and John Cennick in Kingswood. Wesley made the rule that these men might expound the Scriptures but not preach, a fine distinction to draw. It soon appeared that Thomas Maxfield was an ardent interpreter of God's word and possessed a sound knowledge of the treasures of salvation. People flocked to hear him and Maxfield soon found himself preaching to the great benefit of the faithful and the conversion of many unbelievers.

As soon as Wesley heard of this he hurried home and going first into his own room found his mother there. She wanted to know at once why he was so agitated and distressed.

'Thomas Maxfield has turned preacher, I find,' Wesley answered. His mother looked at him searchingly, and said: 'John, you know what my sentiments have been. You cannot suspect me of favouring readily any thing of this kind. But take care what you do with respect to that young man, for he is as surely called of God to preach as you are. Examine what have been the fruits of his preaching: and hear him also yourself.'

This wise advice Wesley decided to follow. True, it was with a certain unwillingness that he sat down to listen to Maxfield, but he was soon convinced, and joyfully exclaimed: 'It is the Lord; let Him do what seemeth Him good.'

With the coming of these new helpers, new visions of the extension of his work opened out before him, and he decided at once to make full use of these men whom God had called. He retained the right to appoint his lay assistants wherever he wished, so that they go where they were needed most. Soon he began to call together the steadily growing band of preachers to consult with him about their work; this was the beginning of the Annual Conference. He also worked out study courses for preachers, for even if they were 'unlearned and ignorant men' who were being sent out with the Gospel, there was no reason why they should remain ignorant. Later he assembled them on different occasions so that they should be even better equipped for their task, and they would sometimes apply to him for help.

John Nelson the Yorkshire stonemason felt in need of Wesley's advice, and begged him as his father in Christ to write and give him some instructions about how he should continue in the work that God had begun with such an unpolished tool as himself.

Wesley answered that he himself would come and visit Nelson the following week. In Birstall he found a flock of ardent Christians who had been converted without his direct work—a flock that had been gathered together by a layman—and his last misgivings about lay preaching disappeared. Lay preaching had forced its way into Methodism, not as an ideal expedient, but more as an emergency principle justifying itself by its results.

While Wesley was riding northwards in 1742 he began to find out that he was already a known and controversial figure. On the way he overtook a man who appeared to be a serious person and Wesley entered into conversation with him. The stranger did not let many minutes pass before he had made clear to Wesley what views he held on matters of faith. In order not to irritate the man Wesley did not answer any particular item in his flood of words. But now the man wanted information on Wesley's own standpoint. 'We had better keep to practical things, lest we should be angry at one another,' said Wesley. So they discussed neutral matters during a ride of several miles, until the stranger caught Wesley off his guard and forced him into a discussion. Becoming even more vehement he declared that Wesley was 'rotten at heart' and that he must surely be one of John Wesley's followers. His companion answered: 'No, I am John Wesley himself.' The man looked as though he had accidentally trodden on a snake, and tried to ride away from Wesley, but the latter 'being the better mounted, kept close to his side' right up to Northampton, still endeavouring 'to show him his heart'.

Newcastle is reputed to have been a beautiful city at this time, with many large and beautiful wooden houses among the brick, extensive parks and broad avenues. The smoke from the factory chimneys had not yet succeeded in blackening this northern city. Wesley found it full of charm and wrote: 'If I did not believe there was another world, I should spend all my summers here, as I know no place in Great Britain comparable to it for pleasantness. But I seek another country, and therefore am content to be a wanderer upon earth.'

But poverty and misery were not lacking in the midst of all this beauty. When Wesley passed through the town for the first time one May day in 1742, he saw many examples of drunkenness and debauchery and heard much cursing and swearing even from children, the like of which he had never heard before. Truly, he said to himself, this place is ripe for anyone coming to call not the righteous but sinners to repentance. He did not find a single person who in his opinion led a serious life.

The following Sunday he went with a friend to Sandgate, the most poverty-stricken part of the town. There they held a meeting at seven o'clock in the morning. After singing the hundredth psalm, Wesley preached. To begin with they had only three or four listeners, but soon the number increased to three or four hundred, and Wesley estimated that there must have been from twelve to fifteen hundred people present before the meeting was over. He preached on 'He was wounded for our transgressions, He was bruised for our iniquities'. People stood gaping and staring at Wesley in deepest astonishment, and he informed them, 'If you desire to know who I am, my name is John Wesley. At five in the evening, with God's help, I design to preach here again.'

When the appointed time came, the whole population was assembled there. Never before had Wesley had such a large gathering. He stood on the top of a little hill and the people gathered around him, the farthest of them being out of earshot. When he had finished preaching, the people swarmed about him and accompanied him to the inn in order to persuade him to remain in the town a while, but Wesley had already promised to return to Birstall.

Not long afterwards Charles, too, came to Newcastle and continued his brother's work with great success, and before the year was out, John also was back in Newcastle and spent six weeks there and in nearby towns. Everywhere people crowded to hear God's word, and the Wesley brothers received a heartwarming welcome. There were many conversions, some accompanied by powerful physical convulsions, but most happening quietly and peacefully. The work in Newcastle found its feet right from the start and it grew steadily.

After many difficulties Wesley bought a site in the town, and then he started to erect a meeting-place, or rather preaching-house, which he himself preferred to call his church. He also started to build a home for orphans, modelled on Francke's foundation in Halle. There was no lack of pessimistic and discouraging prophets. Some said it would never be finished, others that Wesley would not survive to see the roof put on. Financial difficulties were indeed pressing; it was estimated that the building would cost seven hundred pounds, and Wesley owned exactly twenty-six shillings when he began this great undertaking. But he did not himself waver. 'I . . . nothing doubt[ed] but, as it was begun for God's sake, He would provide what was needful for the finishing it.'

When things seemed to be at their worst, God put it into the mind of a Quaker to send Wesley one hundred pounds. Now the work could proceed. The home could provide for forty children and male and female teachers were appointed. At this time when education was unknown, the Sunday-school taught a thousand pupils each week. It was no wonder that Wesley was much loved in Newcastle and many of the miners who had heard him speak in the evening lay down to sleep on benches on the premises so that they could be sure of hearing him next morning. When he left the town after his second visit the affectionate send-off showed the place he had won for himself in the hearts of the people.

When Wesley rode southwards to Epworth for the first time after his evangelical conversion, he put up at an inn wondering whether anyone would happen to recognize him again. A maidservant from the old parsonage was now employed at the inn and it was not long before she greeted him joyfully. Wesley asked: 'Do you know any in Epworth who are in earnest to be saved?' 'I am,' she answered, 'by the grace of

God; and I know I am saved through faith.' It turned out that there were several others with this experience at Epworth and several more who were anxious to feel God's peace in their lives. This knowledge made Wesley's first Saturday evening in Epworth a happy one.

The last time he had been there he had come to confer with his mother about the journey to Georgia. The parsonage was now occupied by Mr Romley the curate, and on Sunday morning, Wesley offered to help him with the service but his offer was declined.

The rumour was soon out over the whole town that Wesley would preach during evensong and the church was crammed with people. But it was Romley who actually gave the sermon. He had chosen the text: 'Quench not the spirit!' One of the surest ways of quenching the spirit was, according to Romley, to become a religious enthusiast, and then 'in a very florid and oratorical manner' he described the Methodists.

But people were not to be disappointed, for as they came out of church one of Wesley's friends gave notice that since Wesley had not received permission to preach in church, it was his intention to speak in the churchyard at six o'clock. When the hour arrived a mighty crowd of listeners had assembled. Wesley stood near the east end of the church and spoke. He stood on his father's gravestone and spoke from there to an assembly that devoured every word he said. There was weeping and emotion in the crowd. Some fell to the ground as though they were dead and many shouted aloud in sorrow for their sins.

Wesley spoke from his father's gravestone every evening for a whole week and the consequences of his preaching seemed to be many and various.

A man who was known to be a decent fellow but to have absented himself from church for thirty years, stood up and listened to Wesley without any change of expression, seeming to be absorbed in his own thoughts. Wesley went up to him and asked him if he were a sinner. 'Sinner enough', answered the man in a deep, rough voice. His weeping family came and fetched him and drove him home. Several years later, Wesley visited this home and from the man's own mouth he learnt that from that hour in the churchyard he had become a new person. Now despite weak health he could still praise God because his soul was cured.

While Wesley was in Epworth he also visited a Justice of the Peace in the neighbourhood. Persecution of Methodists had already begun and people had driven whole waggon-loads of Methodists to him for him to judge. The Justice, however, displayed a courage and liberal-mindedness that was uncommon in that period. When he asked the zealous 'orthodox' why they had brought these people to him they found it hard to give a reason, for they had been carried away by the kind of momentary impulse which directs the behaviour of so many mobs. Finally one of the accusers managed to find an answer. He declared to the magistrate that these people pretended to be better than other people and that they prayed from morning till night.

'But have they done nothing besides?' asked the magistrate.

'Yes, sir,' said an old man, 'an't please your worship, they have *convarted* my wife. Till she went among them, she had such a tongue! And now she is as quiet as a lamb.'

'Carry them back, carry them back,' replied the Justice, 'and let them convert all the scolds in the town.'

One of the company at Wesley's first meeting in Epworth was his brother-in-law John Whitelamb, now parish minister in Wroot. He had helped old Samuel Wesley with the big book on Job and had later been John's pupil in Oxford. Molly Whitelamb was perhaps the only one of Wesley's sisters who was happily married, but unfortunately she died after only ten months' happiness. Whitelamb wrote a letter to Wesley after the meeting which testifies to both his great modesty and his scepticism about Wesley's method of work.

'I saw you at Epworth,' he wrote, 'Fain would I have spoken to you, but that I am quite at a loss how to address you. Your way of thinking is so extraordinary that your presence creates awe, as if you were an inhabitant of another world.

'God grant you, and your followers, may always have entire liberty of conscience. Will not you allow others the same? Indeed, I cannot think as you do, any more than I can help honouring and loving you. . . . The sight of you moves me strangely. . . .

'Dear Sir, is it in my power to serve or oblige you any way? Glad I should be, that you would make use of me. God open all our eyes, and lead us into Truth, whatever it be.'

Wesley availed himself of his brother-in-law's offer and preached both morning and evening in the church at Wroot, where he had been his father's curate during two storm-filled but happy years of youth. The little church could not nearly hold all the people who wanted to get in.

Yet once more he was preaching in Epworth. He carried on for three hours and it was difficult to break off. Wesley had come back to his own neighbourhood and he was to remain in their hearts for good.

But he took no credit for this himself. Listen to the beautiful and justified token of recognition he paid to his father for his work up here in the North: 'Let none think his labour of love is lost because the fruit does not immediately appear!' He later wrote: 'Near forty years did my father labour here, but he saw little fruit of all his labour. I took some pains among this people too, and my strength also seemed spent in vain; but now the fruit appeared. There were scarce any in the town on whom either my father or I had taken any pains formerly; but the seed, sown so long since, now sprung up, bringing forth repentance and remission of sins.'

But if Wesley had won over the townspeople he had not won over Romley the curate. When Wesley later returned to Epworth, some of the Methodists intimated that they intended to come to the Lord's Supper on Sunday. To which Romley replied: 'Pray tell Mr Wesley I shall not give *him* the sacrament, for he is not fit.'

Humility and a sad irony are mingled in Wesley's comment: 'How wise a God is our God! There could not have been so fit a place under heaven, where this should befall me first, as my father's house, the place of my nativity, and the very place where, "according to the straitest sect of our religion", I had so long "lived a Pharisee"! It was also fit, in the highest degree, that he who repelled me from that very table, where I had myself so often distributed the bread of life, should be one who owed his all in this world to the tender love which my father had shown to his, as well as personally to himself.'

But before this last sad happening in Epworth Wesley had experienced another, the death of his mother. He came back from one of his journeys round the country to find his mother 'on the borders of eternity'. She knew no fear or doubt and had only one single wish: to leave this world to be with Christ. The third day after Wesley returned, he could see that the end was near. He sat down by the side of the bed. She had already started her last battle, and could no longer speak, but those present had the impression that she could understand what was going on. Her look was quiet and serene, and her eyes were turned upwards as if she were giving up her soul into God's hands. From three to four o'clock 'the silver cord of life was loosing, and the wheel breaking at the cistern'. And then, suddenly—without struggle or sigh—her soul was released. She was in the land for which she had yearned, and whither she had so devotedly led her children.

Charles was travelling when his mother died, but John and five of his sisters—all the survivors of the flock of children from the old rectory—were gathered round the bed to watch their mother's departure on her last journey. Life and adversity had marked them, but they had learnt to meet hardship or prosperity with the same peace of mind. Her last request to them had been: 'Children, as soon as I am released, sing a psalm of praise to God.' As they carried out her last wish, they had every reason to thank God for such a mother.

Susanna Wesley was buried on 1st August 1742, in Bunhill Fields near the Foundery. Wesley himself describes the scene: 'Almost an innumerable company of people being gathered together, about five in the afternoon I committed to the earth the body of my mother, to sleep with her fathers. The portion of Scripture from which I afterwards spoke was, "I saw a great white throne, and Him that sat on it. . . ." It was one of the most solemn assemblies I ever saw, or expect to see on this side eternity.'

From the home which she shared with John at the Foundery, Susanna Wesley had joined heart and soul in the ever-growing movement of revival and identified herself with the Methodist people. In the early days of the revival she had met God in a way that was quite new for her. At a communion service, when her son-in-law Westley Hall handed her the chalice with the words, 'The blood of our Lord Jesus Christ which was given for thee,' she felt the words strike through her heart and knew that God for Christ's sake had forgiven her all her sins.

The devout and God-fearing woman after seventy years of strict observance and untiring service was towards the end of her life to enjoy a delight in God and an assurance of salvation unknown before, and her son Charles commemorated this revelation in a poem he inscribed on her tombstone.

The relationship between Susanna and her son John was remarkably close. Her opinions mattered a great deal to John Wesley even after he was grown-up; she had stood by his side during the difficult period when the breach with Fetter Lane became necessary, with her independent Dissenting blood she had encouraged him to allow Thomas Maxfield to preach, and her own dauntless and fearless independence left its mark on his character.

She who was so quiet and modest likewise had a decisive influence on his ideal of womankind. It was for his mother that John wrote down the story of his love-affair with Sophy Hopkey in Georgia, and perhaps rejection of her can be traced to her unlikeness to Susanna.

Would he ever be happy with anyone else?

Chapter XVI

Itinerant Preacher

IN A NOT very sympathetic biography of Wesley by Marjorie Bowen, *Wrestling Jacob*, it is stated that 'Wesley can be reckoned among the last of the great English personalities who used Christianity for purposes of self-development'. It is true that it was through Christianity that Wesley's powers reached their fullest expansion. In working on behalf of God's kingdom he found use for every potentiality of his nature. He was preacher and thinker, journalist and organizer, builder and poet, every hour of the day and every day of the year. Tirelessly and with a good grace he employed his rich capacity for work in the service of God.

But if during this work he developed his abundant personality and realized the ideals that were planted in him from childhood, it was accomplished only by complete self-denial. Like Peter, Wesley was to be carried 'whither he would not'.

When later he met malice, narrow-mindedness, slander, and envious criticism from people in every respect lower than he, it is not surprising that in a moment of weakness he could cry out, '*Vitae me redde priori!* [Give me back my former life]. Let me be again an Oxford Methodist', in an ordered and regular life among university folk and congenial people. When someone expressed surprise at his willingness to carry on his exhausting life of continual journeying, he answered: 'True, it is not easy for flesh and blood, and I should not do it did I not believe that there was another life.'

It is precisely in this itinerant existence that we see Wesley in his greatest self-denial and his greatest self-development.

When Wesley at Whitefield's instigation travelled to Bristol to take over his work with the open-air meetings, a journey began that was destined to last almost unbroken for forty years. Fifty times Wesley sailed across the Irish Channel to Ireland, a journey that in the age of sailing ships could claim much more time than nowadays. On foot, on horseback, by coach, on ferries, or in sailing ships, he journeyed in England, Scotland, Ireland, and the Channel Islands.

The total distance that he covered amounted to about two hundred and fifty thousand miles, which is about eighteen or nineteen miles a day, Sundays and week-days, for as many years as his itinerant life continued.

Meanwhile, he wrote two hundred and thirty-one books and delivered about forty thousand sermons. These figures, do not, perhaps, tell us a great deal, but they do nevertheless give us some idea of the amount of work Wesley managed to get through.

Few of Wesley's contemporaries could have known England's highways and byways as well as he. He slept and ate with people of all social classes and income groups throughout the length and breadth of the land and knew the countryside in all weathers and all seasons. He shared the feelings of his age for the beauty of well-laid parks and gentle pastoral landscapes, but he abhorred mountains, which he considered savage and an obstruction to the view.

But all he experienced of the life of the people and nature, was of secondary importance compared with his great objective: 'To spread Scriptural holiness throughout the land.'

Wesley sometimes travelled on foot. While still at school at Charterhouse he kept in training for walking and running, in his student days he had walked from Epworth to Oxford, and discovered even then that some twenty-five miles is a fair day's march. He discovered, too, that it was possible to combine the journey with something useful: he read as he walked. In Georgia he was accustomed to journeying on foot and living in the open-air. When his greatest work now began, he found a use for his ability to walk without getting tired.

It was on horseback, however, that Wesley covered the greatest distances. He was an able horseman even if he did not look very elegant in the saddle; his 'style' had been ruined by sitting with a book in front of his eyes while he rode. He was determined that no time should be wasted, so he let the horse trot along with slack reins while his mind roamed through the realms of thought. On horseback he got through important historical and theological works, and he wrote telling analyses and criticisms of books he had read on horseback and printed them in his *Journal*.

The average distance he covered was something under twenty miles a day, but one occasion he travelled ninety, riding for twenty hours at a stretch with a change of horses on the way. He had as much trouble with his horses as a motorist has with an old car. Incompetent smiths could shoe horses in a way that made them lame, and it could even happen that a horse would lie down and die for no apparent reason.

Wesley took great care of his horse, one of God's creatures and a true helper in the propagation of the gospel. He impressed upon his preachers that their first care must be for their horses when, tired and muddy, they reached the place where they were to spend the night. Wesley had a moving testimony to the fact that God was interested in his horse. One dark day when he had a headache and his horse had gone lame, he thought to himself: 'Cannot God heal either man or beast by any means, or without any? Immediately my weariness and headache ceased, and my horse's lameness in the same instant. Nor did he halt any more that day or the next.'

The *Journal* gives many instances of his being near death. Once when Wesley was riding near Bristol, a waggon came full speed down a hill, crashing into the flank of Wesley's horse with such force that it was thrown to the ground and Wesley shot over its head into a wall. All the same he completed his journey and found when he reached Bristol late in the evening that rumour had it that he was dead! He knew what to do, however, with this assortment of bumps and bruises. 'Some warm treacle took away all the pain in an hour, and the lameness in a day or two.'

When Wesley began his itinerant life there were no good highways in England and coaches went no farther north than York. In many parts of the North they had never even seen a gig or a landau. Journeys could therefore be quite burdensome:

'Many a rough journey have I had before', he records, 'but one like this I never had; between wind, and hail, and rain, and ice, and snow, and driving sleet, and piercing cold. But it is past: those days will return no more, and are, therefore, as though they had never been.'

'Wed.[nesday] 18. Our servant came up and said, "Sir, there is no travelling today. Such a quantity of snow has fallen in the night that the roads are quite filled up." I told him, "At least we can walk twenty miles a day, with our horses in our hands." So in the name of God we set out. The North-east wind was piercing as a sword, and had driven the snow into such uneven heaps that the main road was unpassable.'

That same go-ahead determination constantly drove him forward despite all difficulties. In 1770, when he was sixty-seven years old, he was in the Highlands in the same winter when three young women had tried to cross some of the mountains and were nearly swallowed by the snow-drifts. Wesley dismounted and leading his horse he trudged along with many diversions and many falls until at last he got through!

An old inn-keeper in the West of England used to tell a story about Wesley when he was eighty-three years old. He was supposed to go to St Ives to preach, but his coachman did not know the way. When they came to a stretch of sand that they had to cross, they found it covered by the tide. A fisherman begged Wesley not to attempt the crossing, but Wesley had fixed the meeting for a certain time, and so he urged on his coachman to 'Take the sea! Take the sea!' It was not long before the horses had to start swimming, and Wesley with the sea spray glistening on his long white hair leaned out of the window to encourage the driver who was fully expecting to be drowned at any moment. 'What is your name, driver?' The man told him it was Peter. 'Peter, fear not: thou shalt not sink.' When they came to land, he found dry clothes for the coachman and then went to the meeting and preached.

It was not foolhardiness and still less exhibitionism that had caused Wesley's urgency, but his exact punctuality. He was scrupulously particular about the time, and suffered if he had to waste five minutes of his time or of his congregation's. He once said to one of Charles's sons: 'Sammy, be punctual. Whenever I am to go to a place, the first thing I do is to get ready; then what time remains is all my own.' If the coachman did not arrive on the dot, he began to go on ahead and the coachman had to catch him up, so that his congregations should never have to wait.

Wesley had to be punctual for he always had to preach in several different places on the same day. It was usually announced in advance that he was coming and the people often came out in crowds to meet him. In his later years it sometimes happened that whole multitudes of people accompanied him from a town where he had been preaching until they met halfway a corresponding crowd of people from the next town where he was going to preach.

The prerequisite for such an itinerant life was obviously an iron constitution. Once he rode over fifty miles to a meeting in Epworth and arrived late on Saturday evening, 'little more tired than when I rose in the morning'. His journeys were not accomplished without dangers of many kinds. He records how he 'set out for Grimsby; but at Ferry we were at a full stop, the boatmen telling us we could not pass the Trent: it was as much as our lives were worth to put from shore before the storm abated. We waited an hour; but, being afraid it would do much hurt if I should disappoint the congregation at Grimsby, I asked the men if they did not think it possible to get to the other shore. They said they could not tell; but if we would venture our lives they would venture theirs. So we put off, having six men, two women, and three horses in the boat. Many stood looking after us on the riverside, in the middle of which we were, when, in an instant, the side of the boat was under water, and the horses and men rolling one over another. We expected the boat to sink every moment; but I did not doubt of being able to swim ashore. The boatmen were amazed, as well as the rest; but they quickly recovered, and rowed for life. And soon after, our horses leaping overboard lightened the boat, and we all came unhurt to land.

'They wondered what was the matter I did not rise (for I lay along in the bottom of the boat); and I wondered too, till, upon examination, I found that a large iron crow[bar], which the boatmen sometimes used, was (none knew how) run through the string of my boot, which pinned me down that I could not stir; so that, if the boat had sunk, I should have been safe enough from swimming any farther.'

But the years did take their toll of Wesley, nevertheless. An accident with his horse made it difficult for him to ride long distances at a stretch, and in his sixty-eighth year some of his friends collected money to buy him a carriage. In this, Wesley had bookshelves fixed so that he could study during his journeys which often lasted ten hours.

When Wesley was seventy-nine years old, he set off in a gig from Portsmouth at two o'clock in the morning and arrived in London in the afternoon.

Perhaps the most dangerous drive he ever had was during a journey to Newcastle in 1774. One of Wesley's preachers and a certain Mr Smith rode alongside the carriage, while Mrs Smith and her two small girls sat inside the carriage with Wesley. At the top of a hill both horses suddenly jumped forward for no explicable reason. The driver fell from his seat and the carriage swerved violently from one side of the road to the other. They narrowly missed a small cart, flew over a narrow bridge and into the gate of a farmyard without touching the gateposts. The gate on the far side of the yard was closed, but the horses and carriage broke through it as if it had been a cobweb, and galloped on through a cornfield. Wesley calmly quietened the frightened children: 'Nothing will hurt you: do not be afraid.' Just as the carriage was approaching the edge of a cliff, Mr Smith managed to overtake them and head off the terrified horses and bring them all to safety.

Wesley often travelled by sea but he was never troubled by sea-sickness. On the journey to and from Georgia he had been very frightened during storms but he was never again afraid in a storm, even though his life might be endangered.

The most troublesome thing about sea journeys at that time was the dependence on a convenient wind. Weeks would pass before it was possible to set sail, and Wesley was often impatient to be off, although he put the time to good use. Once he had lain for weeks in port waiting for a wind to take him to Ireland. He took a turn on land in order to hold a meeting, but scarcely had he turned his back when the wind changed and the boat sailed away without him. When the ship was at sea, he never let the opportunity pass without holding services for the passengers and crew, and trying to speak with them individually about God.

The food was often poor when he was travelling. A long day's travelling and preaching in Cornwall during which no food passed his lips concluded with a sermon to the local Methodist society on the text: 'Beware of covetousness.'

He did not always fare better in finding lodgings for the night. On one occasion Wesley and his fellow-preacher John Nelson had nothing better to lie on than the floor. Wesley used his frock-coat for his pillow and Nelson used Burkitt's *Expository Notes on the New Testament* for his. After he had slept thus for three weeks, Wesley, turning over one morning, found that Nelson was awake, too. He slapped him on the shoulder and said: 'Brother Nelson, let us be of good cheer, I have one whole side yet; for the skin is off but on one side.' Good humour was indeed a necessary part of the equipment of an itinerant preacher.

Chapter XVII

The Preacher

IT HAS been estimated that Wesley delivered some forty thousand sermons in the course of his life. He himself supplies a figure of about eight hundred a year. Clearly the majority of these sermons must have been given before relatively small gatherings. True he often preached at five o'clock in the morning and even if the rhythm of day and night at that time was somewhat different from the present day when we have electric light, there were nevertheless quite a few people who, awakened to Christianity and now personally involved in the propagation of the Word, were prepared to gather together at this early hour.

He also of course spoke to large gatherings and possessed in uncommon measure the ability to hold the interest of his audience. Once a crowd of people were sitting on a wall listening to him speak when suddenly the wall collapsed. No one shrieked and few withdrew their attention, unwilling to lose a single word of the preacher. Wesley held his audience without cultivating rhetoric as such. It is said of Whitefield that his sermons never reached their full power until he had preached them fifty or sixty times. On the other hand he is reported to have been able to say the word 'Mesopotamia' in such a way that his audience were moved to tears. There was little affinity in the pulpit styles of these two great preachers. Wesley's comment in 1750 is a disarming one, and reveals something of his own standards as well as of Whitefield's. 'I read prayers, and Mr Whitefield preached. How wise is God in giving different talents to different preachers! Even the little improprieties both of his language and manner were a means of profiting many who would not have been touched by a more correct discourse, or a more calm and regular manner of speaking.'

Wesley's style has been characterized as very simple, but this simplicity was the result of years of intellectual discipline. The story about young Wesley delivering a sermon before a rural gathering is well known. His discourse was couched in words which though high-sounding, were unintelligible to his simple hearers who sat with blank faces and open mouths comprehending nothing. At his second attempt some of the difficult words were omitted and the gathering was now only half-gaping. Determined, however, to shut their mouths completely, he read his sermons first to an intelligent maidservant who agreed to stop him every time he came to a word she did not understand. She shouted 'Stop, Sir!' so often that Wesley became quite impatient, but he schooled himself thereafter to express himself clearly and simply and was rewarded by the knowledge that now the congregation could understand what he said and respond to his message. He often had to break off his sermons because people in the congregation rejoicing in God's presence shouted aloud: 'Hallelujah!' and 'Praise the Lord!' and Wesley tells how 'their usual token of approbation (which somewhat surprised me at first) was clapping me on the back'.

In an entry in his *Journal* for the year 1765 we see where Wesley found the model for his particular style of preaching: 'In the evening I began expounding the deepest part of the Holy Scripture, namely, the first Epistle of St John, by which, above all other, even inspired writings, I advise every young preacher to form his style. Here are sublimity and simplicity together, the strongest sense and the plainest language! How can any one that would "speak as the oracles of God" use harder words than are found here?'

Wesley deprecated Whitefield's mannerisms, and it is clear that Whitefield's oratorical style was strongly dramatic. Wesley could not himself escape the charge of being theatrical. Horace Walpole on one occasion heard Wesley preach when he was an old man. From his none too friendly attitude towards Methodism in general and Wesley in particular comes the following sentence:

'Wondrous clever, but as evidently an actor as Garrick. He spoke his sermon, but so fast, and with so little accent, that I am sure he has often uttered it, for it was like a lesson. There were parts and eloquence in it; but, towards the end, he exalted his voice, and acted very ugly enthusiasm.'

This is how an antagonist saw him. Wesley's close friend, Henry Moore, says that the first time he heard Wesley preach, he marvelled that this man had been able to create such an aura around himself. But he remembered more of this sermon than of any other he had ever heard.

Wesley's posture in the pulpit was easy and unaffected and his movements quiet and natural. He wore clerical garb even when he spoke in the open air. His voice was not loud but was manly and strong and it could be heard a hundred and fifty yards away. He urged his preachers to guard against shouting; this he never did, though he would occasionally raise his voice to emphasize the point and strike home the decisive blow. He could be carried away by the inspiration of the moment. Once when he was preaching, he suddenly broke off his clear, logical exposition of the text and cried out: ' "Lord, is Saul also among the prophets? Is James Watson here? If he be, show Thy power!" Down dropped James Watson like a stone, and began crying aloud for mercy.'

He lived to see God's Word become a fire and a hammer. The power of God's spirit was made manifest and was not to be quenched. Time and again he was ready to close but could not, sometimes preaching for three hours at a time. But generally he did not preach for more than one hour and towards the end of his life for only half an hour, and his preachers had instructions to preach no longer than one hour.

Wesley usually delivered his sermons just as he had written them and advised his preachers to do the same. 'Carry out what you intend!'

Wesley's biographer, Telford, tells how Wesley delivered his first sermon without preparation. That was in 1739, when the clergyman appointed to preach did not turn up at the church. When people saw Wesley in the congregation they persuaded him to preach, but as he made his way to the pulpit, his courage deserted him. Crestfallen, he went into the vestry where the female verger asked him what was wrong. When Wesley complained that he had no sermon with him, she put her hand on his shoulder and said: 'Is that all? Can not you trust God for a sermon?' Going into the church again he preached easily and well. Later he was never dependent upon manuscript, and did not even take notes with him into the pulpit.

The logical construction of his sermons made them easy listening. This former lecturer in logic, had obviously little to learn about that. His style may at first seem unfamiliar to the modern reader, but the sermons are soon found to capture attention with their convincing thought, solid and orthodox interpretation of the Bible, and practical utility. Compared with the rest of the sermon literature we have from Wesley's time, they stand in a class by themselves.

We possess one hundred and forty-one sermons from Wesley's hand. Most of them were printed in his *Arminian Magazine*, later called the *Methodist Magazine*. Many were published independently, often with one or more of Charles Wesley's hymns on the same theme as the sermon. These printed sermons have been read by Methodists on both sides of the Atlantic for the past two hundred years and have been a constant source of inspiration for Methodist preaching. An appointed selection of these sermons—some forty-four—is one of the Methodist standards of doctrine and they must be studied by all candidates for the Methodist ministry.

The published sermons contain few illustrations, no far-fetched interpretation or sensationalism. There are no sops to bad taste or popular acclaim. In an age that was sentimental and judged a book or sermon according to its power to stimulate the lachrymal glands, Wesley is blessedly sober and factual.

It has been maintained that a good theologian can be recognized by the fact that he appreciates the distinction between Law and Gospel, and in this sense, Wesley was a great theologian. He preached God's message and God's will with great penetration and power. When men had once awakened to the realization of sin, he could preach God's forgiving grace and love so that his hearers' lives were transformed.

Some of Wesley's friends were sometimes embarrassed by his choice of text. He could, for instance, address a gathering of wealthy and important people on Jesus's scathing words to the Pharisees: 'Vipers, who taught you to flee from the wrath to come?' Such texts should be used in the slum quarters of Billingsgate, they said. 'Oh, no,' Wesley answered, 'there I shall preach on: "Behold what manner of love the Father hath bestowed upon us, that we should be called children of God".'

Wesley's preaching went deep into people's consciousness because of his direct application of Christian teaching to moral and practical living. He declared that men could be literally set free from sin and their lives made new.

Wesley once heard an artistic and elaborate sermon up in Scotland, but he thought it would be no more effective than the song of a lark because it had no sting, no direct application to life itself. Wesley assessed the presentation of the Christian faith in books and sermons from the point of view of its practical results. He asked of each: Does it bring sinners to conversion and a personal life in the service of God? Is it designed to give assurance of salvation and is it a path to Christian activity and a holy life? Everything else was but the warbling of a lark to Wesley.

His preaching never led men into a sort of fools' paradise, a cloud-cuckoo land in which everything was made easy for the believer. Fearlessly Wesley preached the gospel of Christian perfection. He had once called John's first epistle the most profound of all New Testament writings, and on this contemplation of Christian love his mind often dwelt, because in it he found a picture of the goal of sanctification.

Chapter XVIII

The Many-headed Monster

IT IS A fact that when people collect in a crowd they do things that no individual in the crowd would ever have dreamt of doing by himself. There is a sort of mass intoxication in which responsibility for the happenings is renounced, and when those taking part in the disorders are called to account for their excesses they can hardly understand how they could ever have taken part in them.

Wesley and all the early Methodist preachers got a first-hand knowledge of the many-headed monster that is called the mob, whether it consisted of the ignorant or the so-called 'upper classes', and in the course of time Wesley became an adept at bringing it into subjection.

The mob was in evidence right from the time of the first open-air meetings, but as time went on it became really troublesome and often dangerous. Riots were one way of passing the time in an age when amusements were scanty, rough, and irresponsible. Youthful exuberance always seeks some outlet and a crowd was easily led by the first mad-cap who came forward with a suggestion for diversion. Wesley's meetings were of a kind that would arouse this sort of thing. They represented something completely new and there were many instances of powerful spiritual ferment. Something *happened* there.

Mobs were also 'lower-class' risings against authority. A clergyman setting himself up at some street corner to preach would necessarily be regarded as somewhat queer. No self-respecting clergyman would behave so. The stones that were cast at the little man in clerical robes and his assistants were unconsciously hurled at all that bore the name of authority and officialdom.

Wesley stood before them in no sense as a political figure; his dominating thought was to win souls for God, but his work had such widespread influence that historians have given him the credit for saving England from a repetition of the excesses of the French Revolution. The New Jerusalem which Wesley envisaged would be built up from free and transformed personalities. 'You have nothing to do but to save souls,' Wesley used to say to his helpers.

Now precisely in this way a new community of men was created in England. They were people who were still among the lower social classes, but they had discovered to their surprise that their lives were set in a larger framework than that of the family. Failure to live up to Christian standards meant expulsion from the society; if they were faithful in small tasks, on the other hand, they would be given large and important duties and be entrusted with the office of class-leaders or local preachers. No longer did they use up their money on drink, dissipation, and gambling; instead they and their families began to enjoy a standard of living impossible before. Socially, therefore, the revival brought in its wake an improvement in living conditions, and psychologically it produced a decided change in outlook on life. All in all the revival became one of the most decisive factors in the political and economic life of England during the century.

Thus, this movement that the mob attacked was to be the cause of raising those worst placed both culturally, socially, economically, and politically.

One of the reasons why so many people made difficulties for Wesley was the fact that the clergy preached against him from their pulpits and gave a distorted impression of his teaching to their congregations. A flood of rumours grew up around Wesley. He was accused both of immoral behaviour and of being a political agitator. The crowd felt resentment against both Dissenters and Catholics and Wesley was variously accused of both. As we know, he considered himself the whole of his life a genuine son of the English Church, and these accusations hit him hard.

Allegations that Wesley was a Catholic were particularly serious because a Pretender of the House of Stuart was actually at this moment assembling troops in the North of France ready for an invasion of England. It was rumoured that Wesley had been seen in the company of the Pretender and that Methodism was an underground movement working on behalf of the Pretender's cause.

The Methodists did in actual fact meet together in small groups and Wesley and his preachers travelled freely over the length and breadth of the land and would have had plenty of opportunity of spying and conspiring. Several of the riots in the South of England had their origin in these fantastic rumours. On one occasion Wesley was arrested and hauled before a court. The magistrate asked him—sheepishly and self-consciously, it is true—whether he was willing to swear fealty to the King. Wesley answered 'Yes' without reflection or reservation.

Other rumours declared that he had been arrested for unlawfully selling gin, that he was a Jesuit, that he had hanged himself, and that the person who claimed to be Wesley was in reality an impostor representing the true Wesley who had died long ago.

Charles had once prayed to God during divine service to 'call home his banished'. This was sufficient instigation for people to begin saying that he had prayed for the exiled Stuarts, and that he was working to get them back. He had to go before a court and give an explanation.

Many were the distractions that might happen while Wesley was preaching. The church bells would begin to ring, drunken fiddlers and singers were hired to play and bawl out songs, and hurdy-gurdies were carried out into the street to drown the voice of the preacher. A drummer might start up near by and play with all his might, trumpeters might suddenly feel an irresistible urge to practise their art close to the meeting-place, or a man might set up his stall and start to cry 'Fresh salmon!' In London itself it even happened that a man tried to drive a herd of cows through the crowd of listeners. 'But the brutes were wiser than their masters,' writes Wesley. 'They went another way.'

But on the same occasion something more serious happened. The crowd started to throw stones. 'They then threw whole showers of stones, one of which struck me just between the eyes: but I felt no pain at all; and, when I had wiped away the blood, went on testifying with a loud voice that God hath given to them that believe "not the spirit of fear, but of power, and of love, and of a sound mind".'

Some of the stones hit people in the crowd, sometimes with most surprising results. A woman was hit between the eyes with a stone, with such force that it laid her on the ground. 'In that same moment all her anger disappeared and only love filled her heart.'

Wesley preserved a healthy respect for stones the whole of his life through. Once he was supposed to be giving an address, but as the room was too small he was shown into a courtyard. 'One circumstance of this I did not like,' he said. 'It was plentifully furnished with stones —artillery ready at hand for the devil's drunken companions.'

In the two main centres of Methodism, London and Bristol, it soon became relatively safe for Wesley. Once, in 1740, he had a large crowd gathered round him at the Foundery, and he gave thanks to God because the opportunity he had so long been awaiting had finally arrived. He spoke gently and insistently to his audience and succeeded in winning their attention. On the following Tuesday many of the trouble-makers attended the meeting and many accepted salvation. 'I wonder the devil has not wisdom enough to discern that he is destroying his own kingdom,' he said. 'I believe he has never yet, any one time, caused this open opposition to the truth of God, without losing one or more of his servants, who were found of God while they sought Him not.' For Wesley there was no doubt that there were Satanic powers at work when the mob was raving. Towards the individuals forming the crowd he was mildly disposed and 'offered them deliverance from their hard master'.

Riots began as early as the revival's first year, but from 1742 they gradually spread over the country and in parts assumed the character of direct persecution. At Wednesbury in Staffordshire some of the most notable persecutions took place. When Wesley visited this town for the first time he met with a hearty welcome, even from the vicar. Later, however, one of his preachers was foolish enough to express open criticism of the vicar, who reacted with a powerful sermon. Popular opinion, however, was still on the side of the Methodists, and when a clergyman from nearby tried to ride down some of those attending the meeting, he was vigorously opposed by those present. Shortly afterwards Charles Wesley found himself able to preach at the opening of a Methodist preaching-house in the town.

But then trouble broke out again for quite a different reason. One of the first Methodists, James Jones, told what happened:

'The mob had been gathering all Monday night, and on Tuesday morning they began their work. They assaulted, one after another, all the houses of those who were called Methodists. They first broke all their windows, suffering neither glass, lead, nor frames to remain therein. Then they made their way in; and all the tables, chairs, chests of drawers, with whatever was not easily removable, they dashed in pieces, particularly shop-goods, and furniture of every kind. What they could not well break, as feather-beds, they cut in pieces and strewed about the room. William Sitch's wife was lying in; but that was all one; they pulled away her bed too, and cut it in pieces.'

Houses were looted and there was no restraint to the violence of the mob.

Some of the gentlemen who had worked up the mob or threatened to dismiss the miners who did not take part in the riot, now drew up a document that all those belonging to the society were to sign, stating that they would never again invite, or entertain any Methodist preacher. On this condition they promised to stop the mob's excesses, otherwise they would have to accept the consequences. They took along this offer to a number of people, but these declared that they had already lost their possessions and had nothing else to lose except their life. Even that would be better than to sin against their conscience.

This persecution of the Methodists continued for six days without anyone interfering. Wesley was so moved by this report that he broke out: 'Tell me, for what sort of payment can we procure men to do this service? to be always afraid of going to prison or meeting death?'

Wesley had received news of this disturbance on a Saturday. As soon as his Sunday meetings in London were over he rushed to Wednesbury to see for himself and, if possible, to be a help and comfort.

Three months later he was in Wednesbury once again.

The day after he arrived he preached in the centre of the town at midday, and for one reason or another nobody interfered, the people possibly being struck dumb by such boldness! At any rate he managed to finish his sermon in peace. But in the afternoon when he was sitting in his room writing, he heard a crowd gathering outside egging one another on. He advised his companions—they must have been brave people—to pray to God. Within an hour the crowd was ready to disperse, but then came reinforcements of more violent elements, and the attack began. They shouted with one voice: 'Bring out the minister; we will have the minister.'

Wesley invited the leader of the crowd into the house and spoke to him. It was not long before the lion became a lamb, and Wesley persuaded him to go out and bring in two or three of his wildest companions. He fetched two who looked furious enough for anything, but they, too, soon calmed down after a short chat with Wesley.

Then Wesley went out to the crowd, climbed on to a chair and said:

'What do you want with me?'

'We want you to go with us to the Justice.'

'That I will with all my heart,' Wesley replied.

Then he delivered a short address to the crowd and some were so moved that they shouted out: 'The gentleman is an honest gentleman, and we will spill our blood in his defence.'

But not all were to be so easily won over and at last Wesley was led away in pouring rain to stand before a magistrate in the presence of a crowd of two or three hundred people.

After these riots the Staffordshire Justices issued a document typical of the times, in effect a standing order for the arrest of all Methodist preachers:

'Whereas we, his Majesty's Justices of the Peace for the said County of Stafford, have received information that several disorderly persons, styling themselves Methodist Preachers, go about raising routs and riots, to the great damage of His Majesty's liege people, and against the peace of our Sovereign Lord the King:

'These are, in his Majesty's name, to command you and every one of you, within your respective districts, to make diligent search after the said Methodist Preachers, and to bring him or them before some of us his said Majesty's Justices of the Peace, to be examined concerning their unlawful doings.'

On this occasion they got not only one of these 'loose persons' but the leader himself hauled before them, priest in Holy Orders and Oxford don, John Wesley. The charge that the crowd brought to the notice of the judge was this: 'They sing psalms all day; nay, and make folks rise at five in the morning.' The first magistrate they approached was wise enough to send down the message that he had gone to bed and that he advised everybody else to do the same. The matter was taken farther, in pouring rain, to a magistrate in the next town. But this was clearly one of those days when authority had gone to bed early, for this justice gave the same information as the other. So it was decided that about fifty youths should accompany Wesley home. This time, strange to tell, they formed a sort of bodyguard for him.

Meanwhile, the rumour had spread in Walsall that John Wesley was there with some people from Wednesbury. This at once set tempers on the boil. The Walsall mob collected under the leadership of some of the worst elements in the town and now began a brawl in which mobs from the two towns fought over who should take charge of Wesley. This was not the first time that the youth of both the towns had measured their strength against one another on just such a pretext as this, but this encounter just missed a serious outcome as it almost cost Wesley his life.

The fight took place outside the town and began about seven o'clock in the evening. The Walsall crowd started off with real energy and had seemingly little difficulty in disposing of the Wednesbury party, many of whom were knocked down and the rest ran away. Wesley was left in the hands of the Walsall crowd like one of the spoils of war; against the shouts of victory it was in vain to attempt to speak.

So they took Wesley back with them to Walsall again. There he tried to slip through a door, but a hand grabbed him by the collar and held him back. He was dragged through the main street from one end of the town to the other, but continued to talk to those nearest him, feeling neither pain nor fatigue. Trying once more to get through a door that stood open, he was refused by the owner who was afraid the crowd would tear the whole place down.

So Wesley took up his position on the steps and asked the crowd: 'Are you willing to hear me speak?'

Many cried out: 'No, no! knock his brains out; down with him; kill him at once.' Others said: 'Nay, but we will hear him first.'

Then Wesley began to address individuals in the crowd and asked them one by one: 'What evil have I done? Which of you all have I wronged in word or deed?'

After speaking to them for more than a quarter of an hour his voice unexpectedly failed him and the crowd took advantage of this to shout again: 'Bring him away! Bring him away!'

Then his voice returned as suddenly as it had left him and he began to pray aloud to God. In a flash the attitude of the leader of the mob underwent a change. He turned to Wesley and said:

'Sir, I will spend my life for you: follow me, and not one soul here shall touch a hair of your head.' Two or three of his companions joined him and the people scattered to right and left while these men took Wesley between them and went like Israel through the Red Sea.

By ten o'clock he was safe and sound in Wednesbury. 'I never saw such a chain of providences before,' Wesley comments.

During the fracas many attempts had been made to knock him over, and on the steep slope he might easily have been trampled to death. A brutish fellow brandished a club at his head, but Wesley's short stature was to his advantage, for many of the blows aimed at him landed on his enemies. He did receive a hard blow on the chest and one on the mouth that drew blood, but he affirmed that he felt no greater pain from that than if they had touched him with a straw. 'From the beginning to the end I found the same presence of mind as if I had been sitting in my own study.'

He had been encircled by God's protection and by the prayers of the friends who were assembled in the house where the uproar had begun.

Wesley's tribulations turned the mood of the town in his favour, and when next day he rode through the town he received many proofs of devotion and love. He had won a victory for truth through an apparent defeat.

Charles met his brother just afterwards in Nottingham and reported that John looked really like a soldier of Christ. His clothes were torn to shreds and he was covered with scars and scratches. Far from warning Charles of danger, he urged him to make his way to Wednesbury and Walsall there and then. It was not his first encounter with the 'fierce Ephesian beasts' as he called them but he did not flinch from a second trial. This time one of the leaders of the mob came to Charles in great distress and consciousness of sin and accepted salvation, and five days after this last riot he was received on trial into the Methodist society.

'What do you really think of my brother?' Charles asked him. 'Think of him?' said he, 'That he is a mon of God; and God was on his side, when so mony of us could not kill one mon.' This former trouble-maker often testified in later life as to how God had saved him from laying hands on the servant of the Lord.

In various parts of the country Methodist homes were broken into and looted. Some of the preachers were seriously wounded, some half-drowned, others rolled in paint. Many women were so ill-treated that they bore the marks for the rest of their lives. All kinds of tortures were inflicted upon fearless and courageous witnesses of God, but by their steadfastness they awakened people's curiosity and later their compassion until finally they were able to lead many of their enemies into a personal experience of God.

In the South of England the Methodists did not so often meet with persecution as they did in the more turbulent and uncultivated Midlands, but here too they were to encounter opposition. It was Charles who took the lion's share of the difficulties in the South. In St Ives in Cornwall he had founded a Methodist society and built a chapel. But opposition was considerable, and when the news came that the English had won an action in Spain, the mob in its joy tore the premises down! 'Such is the Cornish method of thanksgiving,' remarked Wesley drily. It was the rumour about Wesley's connexion with the Catholic Pretender that lingered in people's minds.

Several of Wesley's preachers were captured by press-gangs, groups of soldiers charged with forcing people into the army or navy against their will. All vagrants ran the risk of being seized by such a gang, and it was relatively easy for the recruiting officers to get their hands on Wesley's preachers. They were not ordained and had no fixed abode but travelled from place to place possessing no other occupation. Wesley was fortunate enough to be able to secure the release of some of them with the help of Lady Huntingdon, a pillar of Whitefield's branch of Methodism, and many of the preachers were set free when they were brought before the military commanders.

Wesley also learnt what it was like to be a 'pressed soldier'. He was standing preaching in the street somewhere in Cornwall when a man came up to him and said: 'Sir, I have a warrant from Dr Borlase, and you must go with me.'

The authorities in those parts thought that they could root out the evil of Methodism if they could force its leader into service abroad. But when Wesley was brought before Dr Borlase, and he saw that he was no wild fanatic but an educated man, he thought better of it and only wanted to extricate himself from the whole affair.

Released in the morning, Wesley was to be apprehended again that same evening. He was preaching in the street of a neighbouring town when a number of men rode past. One of them caught sight of Wesley and shouted: 'Seize him! Seize him! I say, seize the preacher for his Majesty's service!' When the order was not obeyed immediately, the man jumped down himself from his horse and caught Wesley by his gown. 'I take you to serve his Majesty,' he announced.

Then he took Wesley by the arm and went off with him declaiming so emphatically the wickedness of the Methodists that he used up all his breath. Wesley availed himself of this opportunity to get in a few words.

'Sir, be they what they will, I apprehend it will not justify you in seizing me in this manner, and violently carrying me away, as you said, to serve his Majesty.'

His challenger replied: 'I seize you! And violently carry you away! No, sir; no. Nothing like it. I asked you to go with me to my house, and you said you was willing; and if so, you are welcome; and if not, you are welcome to go where you please.'

'Sir, I know not if it would be safe for me to go back through this rabble.'

'Sir, I will go with you myself.'

Wesley continues in his *Journal*: 'He then called for his horse, and another for me, and rode back with me to the place from whence he took me.'

Such scenes could be annoying enough, but for all that, they were not without humour. Far more serious was what happened next day at Falmouth. Wesley was staying with a woman who was a cripple when the mob collected outside her house shouting: 'Bring out the canorum! Where is the canorum?' ('Canorum', the name used in Cornwall for Methodists, probably referred to their hearty singing.) The mob now broke in through the door and entered the hall. The people who lived in the house had all gathered together for safety except Wesley and an old serving woman who wanted Wesley to hide himself in a cupboard. Wesley himself realized that his life was in extreme danger but was sure that to hide would only make matters worse and he made it a rule to look the mob straight in the face. The party-wall soon broke under their onslaught and he faced them with the words: 'Here I am. Which of you has anything to say to me? To which of you have I done any wrong? To you? Or you? Or you?' In this way he approached the crowd as responsible individuals.

'I continued speaking till I came, bareheaded as I was (for I purposely left my hat, that they might all see my face), into the middle of the street, and then, raising my voice, said, "Neighbours, countrymen! Do you desire to hear me speak?" They cried vehemently: "Yes, yes. He shall speak. He shall. Nobody shall hinder him." . . . I never saw . . . the hand of God so plainly shown as here; . . . although the hands of perhaps some hundreds of people were lifted up to strike or throw, yet they were one and all stopped in the mid-way; so that not a man touched me with one of his fingers; neither was anything thrown from first to last; so that I had not even a speck of dirt on my clothes.'

This remark about 'a speck of dirt on my clothes' reveals incidentally something of Wesley's fastidiousness and sense of order. But there were far more vital things at stake than a speck of dirt.

Wesley had a special gift of changing the mood of an unruly meeting. In Bolton he declared: 'Such rage and bitterness I scarce ever saw before, in any creatures that bore the form of men.' Those who had been present at the meeting accompanied him home and the streets were full of excited people. Wesley and his friends got back to the house, but when one of them tried to leave he was rolled in the mud until he was scarcely recognizable. The ringing of a bell gave notice of an attack, and Wesley came downstairs to find the whole of the ground floor full of people who had pressed in from the street. Wesley asked for a chair, and at once 'The winds were hushed, and all was calm and still. My heart was filled with love, my eyes with tears, and my mouth with arguments. They were amazed, they were ashamed, they were melted down, they devoured every word. What a turn was this! Oh how did God change the counsel of the old Ahithophel into foolishness; and bring all the drunkards, swearers, Sabbath-breakers, and mere sinners in the place, to hear of His plenteous redemption!'

The next morning at five o'clock the chapel was packed to suffocation and Wesley preached considerably longer than usual, but the people clamoured for more, so he promised to preach again at nine o'clock on an open space outside the town. His hearers came crowding together. 'Oh how have a few hours changed the scene! We could now walk through every street of the town, and none molested or opened his mouth, unless to thank or bless us.'

On another occasion an all-too-zealous member of the mob forced his way into the house where Wesley was and then discovered to his horror that he could not get out again and that he was himself a target for the stones of the crowd. A blow on the forehead caused him to shout: 'O, sir, are we to die tonight? What must I do? What must I do?' Wesley said: 'Pray to God. He is able to deliver you from all danger.' He began praying 'in such a manner as he had scarce done ever since he was born'.

Once Wesley, after a meeting in a barn, came out to find that the carriage in which he was to have travelled had gone. Some of those who had been present at the meeting offered Wesley a seat in their carriage even though it was already full. The crowd now started to hurl anything they could find at the carriage windows, but he said, 'A large gentlewoman who sat in my lap screened me, so that nothing came near me.'

There was not much danger that these excesses of the mob would be punished. One of Wesley's preachers, John Hampson, felt that vengeance was too long delayed and took the matter into his own hands. To Wesley's protest he replied: 'Let me alone, sir; if God has not given you an arm to quell this mob, He has given me one, and the first man who molests you here, I will lay him dead.' The threat did not perhaps become a preacher's mouth, but it was at least effective.

It was some time before the authorities began to recognize that the Methodists had human rights. At first they did not even take action if a Methodist chapel were torn down over the heads of the worshippers. A Methodist who asked for justice because his house had been robbed was answered like this: 'Thou conceited fellow, art thou too turned religious? They may burn thy house if they will; thou shalt have no justice.'

Gradually, however, things improved. When Wesley was stopped in a street in Newcastle and abused in the hearing of many bystanders, he sent his detractor a sharp letter and threatened to report him. A few hours later the man turned up and politely begged for forgiveness.

It is worth while to note that the king himself at the very start of the persecutions had given orders that the Methodists should be protected. A Quaker who had once been an Oxford Methodist and who was a very respected and influential man was asked by the king if he had met the Wesley brothers while he was at Oxford. He added: 'They make a great noise in the nation.'

The Quaker replied: 'I know them well, King George; and thou mayest be assured, that thou hast not two better men in thy dominions, nor men that love thee better, than John and Charles Wesley.'

As Wesley's life and work went on, these outbreaks ceased altogether, and he met with touching affection everywhere he went. By his steadfastness, determination, and Christian love he triumphed over the many-headed monster who had threatened to crush both him and the movement he had created. Indeed he did much to transform the ignorant mass whom no one had ever bothered about, and the mob listened attentively to the man who had come not to call the righteous but sinners to repentance. Many obeyed the call and became respectable and disciplined members of society, and what is more, happy Christians.

Chapter XIX

Wesley's Last Love

ANY ACCOUNT of John Wesley would be incomplete without the story of his love for Grace Murray. The woman he loved and who seemed in many ways to be marked out to become his wife was thirteen years younger than Wesley. When she was only sixteen her parents wanted to marry her off to a man much older than herself, and Grace Norman ran away from home to her elder sister's. After she had been there for a month, she went into domestic service, a step which had some influence on her future, for in the view of the age this lowly station unfitted her to be the wife of a minister. A few years later she married a ship's captain, Alexander Murray.

While Wesley was still in Georgia enduring all the disappointments and sorrows of his relationship with Sophy Hopkey, Grace was in England, happily married to a man as unlike John Wesley as it was possible to be. Alexander Murray had no religious interests and no inhibitions. Their first child, called Grace, died, and this sorrow made the bereaved mother turn towards God. One day she and her husband saw a strange clergyman preaching on Kensington Common, and Grace was anxious to stop and listen to this George Whitefield, but Murray was not in the mood for listening and hurried her on.

Another son was born to Grace and he was a great comfort to her while her husband was away at sea, but this child also died and for a time she went through a serious spiritual crisis. She felt that God was punishing her because she had not accepted Him, and her grief and sense of guilt almost drove her out of her mind. Her sisters tried to get her to go dancing to liven her up, but in vain. Then she heard of something much better: open-air meetings at Moorfields early in the morning.

She lay awake the whole of the night and was up again by four, ready to go to the meeting with another woman. They found quite a large company assembled there to seek their Saviour, many who were cast down by sin and guilt and whose spiritual conflict was a hard one.

In the quiet of the morning a ringing voice was heard. It was not theatrical or declamatory, but sober, matter of fact, and convincing. It came from a man with dark-brown hair, slight in build and dressed in clerical garb. His glance was imperious, but also gentle. He proclaimed to the gathering, 'Except a man be born again, he cannot see the Kingdom of God', and he went on to plead with his hearers to come to a settlement with God. Hope began to dawn in her soul. Was it really possible to be saved? And was it possible for her?

The hardness of her heart was broken and Grace accepted God's offer of love there and then.

Soon after this Alexander Murray returned home from sea and did not at all like the new state of affairs, feeling that he was opposed by forces he could not understand. A supernatural power was rival for his wife's love, and he thought she must have gone out of her mind. He threatened to send her to a madhouse if she did not stop associating with the Methodists. But Grace held on to what she had discovered even though her husband now threatened desertion: 'If you are resolv'd to go on thus, I will leave you: I will go as far as ships can sail.'

She answered quietly: 'I cannot help it; I could lay down my life for you. But I cannot destroy my soul. If you are resolv'd to go, you must go; I give you up to God.'

Alexander Murray then set off on a voyage during which he died. The night in 1742 on which he perished, Grace dreamed of this very occurrence. 'When I waked, I was convinc'd my Husband was dead. But I was so fill'd with God, that at this time nothing could disturb or interrupt my happiness in Him. . . . I felt the everlasting Arms were round me.'

New tasks now took up her time. Grace joined the Methodists, and John Wesley, through whose preaching she had first found God, appointed her as class-leader, 'band' leader, and sick visitor and nurse. She was next to be made housekeeper of his children's home in Newcastle.

There arose certain differences of opinion between her and the rest of the staff of the orphanage, but in 1745 we find her once again serving the Methodists in London. She was now a sort of nurse for sick and worn-out preachers and had at least seven of them to care for. It was during this period that Wesley found in Grace Murray the qualities of neatness and order which he prized so highly.

In 1748 he himself was taken ill in Newcastle with a high fever. Throughout a long and restless night he had plenty of opportunity to appreciate her kindly and capable handling of the sick. Perhaps Charles's approaching marriage also influenced John and he told Grace Murray that if ever he were to marry, she would be the woman for him.

To Grace Murray this man who somewhat hesitatingly offered her his hand was one of England's leading figures. Abused, ridiculed and wronged, his name had been on everyone's lips. But now he was well on the way to gaining general regard and it was this man of God who now offered her his hand.

Grace remembered on the other hand her own modest past, and even if she had shown herself a willing and useful servant of Christ who had brought many to God, she still realized the magnitude of this offer, and her answer was: 'This is too great a blessing for me: I can't tell how to believe it. This is all I could have wish'd for under Heaven, if I had dar'd to wish for it.'

Wesley used to tell his preachers that they ought not to preach one sermon the less or travel a mile the less even though they were married. He carried out his own advice in his courtship of Grace Murray and the greater part of the time that they were together was spent in prayer and meditation. They had little enough time together as the demands of the work kept them apart. After his illness Wesley soon returned to God's battlefield and would not comply with her entreaties to shorten his absence from her. He told her however: 'I am convinc'd God has call'd you to be my Fellow-labourer in the Gospel. I will take you with me to Ireland in Spring. Now we must part for a time. But, if we meet again, I trust we shall part no more.'

Two years earlier Grace had nursed through a long and dangerous illness one of Wesley's most capable preachers, John Bennet, a man of substance and education. They had continued to write to one another but there was no matrimonial engagement between them. When Wesley set out with Grace on a preaching tour through Yorkshire he took her to Bennet's home and asked him to take good care of Mrs Murray. Bennet wanted to know if there was anything finally settled between herself and Wesley and she told him there was not. Not long after she promised to marry Bennet, and both of them wrote to Wesley about the matter. Grace's own statement was that she was sure that this marriage was God's will. Thinking that they were already man and wife, Wesley was amazed and wrote a gentle letter back to them. Grace's reply was so devoted and tender that Wesley next got the impression that the plan had been given up. When they met again, she convinced Wesley that she had not been able to believe in his proposal. 'Till now all this had seem'd to her as a dream, nor could she possibly think, what I propos'd would ever come to pass.'

Grace now joined Wesley and some others on a journey to Bristol, afterwards attending Charles's wedding to Sarah Gwynne in Wales, and later they travelled with some other preachers to Ireland where they stayed several months. Wesley reported of his friend and helper: 'I saw the Work of God prosper in her hands. She lightened my Burden more than can be exprest. She examin'd all the Women in the smaller Societies and the Believers in every place. . . . Meantime she was to me both a Servant and Friend, as well as a Fellow-labourer in the Gospel. She provided everything I wanted.' Before returning from Ireland they had entered into a solemn agreement that was tantamount to an engagement.

Wesley had not wooed Grace Murray from any sudden impulse but had considered the whole matter in great detail. When he was little, he used to amuse his friends by saying that he would never marry anyone until he found someone who was as good as his mother. This principle influenced him subconsciously, while at the conscious level the decisive factor was the priority of God's work.

When now Wesley had thought the matter out very carefully, and weighed the arguments for and against marriage, he found he had seven objections to matrimony. The lecturer in logic gathered them all together for careful examination and one by one brilliantly overcame all objections and doubts. The list is revealing of the character of its author as well as the character of its subject.

'First, as a Housekeeper, She has every qualification I desire. She understands all I want to have done. She is remarkably neat in person, in cloaths, in all things. She is nicely frugal, yet not sordid. She has much Common Sense: contrives every thing for the best; makes every thing go as far as it can go; Foresees what is wanting and provides it in time; does all things quick and yet without hurry. She is a good Workwoman; able to do the finest, ready to do the coarsest Work; Observes my Rules, when I am absent as well as when I am present: And takes care, that those about her observe them, yet seldom disobliges any of them.

'As a Nurse, (which my poor, shatter'd infeebled Carcase now frequently stands in need of) She is careful to the last degree, indefatigably patient, and inexpressibly tender. She is quick, cleanly, skilful, and understands my Constitution better than most Physicians.

'As a Companion, she has Good Sense, and some Knowledge both of books and men. She is of an engaging Behaviour, and of a mild, sprightly, chearful, and yet serious Temper.

'As a Friend, She has been long tried and found faithfull. She watches over me both in Body and Soul; understanding all my Weaknesses, sympathizing with me and helpfull to me in all: Never ashamed, never afraid: Having a continual Presence of mind, in all Difficulties and Dangers: In all enabled to cover my head and strengthen my hands in God.

'Lastly, as a Fellow Labourer in the Gospel of Christ (the light wherein my Wife is to be chiefly consider'd) She had in a measure which I never found in any other both Grace and Gifts and Fruit. With regard to the first; She is crucified to the world, desiring nothing but God, dead to the Desire of the Flesh, the Desire of the Eye, the

Pride of Life: Exemplarily chast, modest, temperate; yet without any Affectation. She is teachable and reprovable; Gentle and longsuffering: Eminently compassionate, weeping with those that weep, bearing both my Burthens, those of the Preachers, and those of the People: Zealous of Good Works, longing to spend and be spent for the Glory of God and the Good of men.

'As to her Gifts, She has a clear Apprehension and a deep Knowledge of the things of God: A quick Discernment of Spirits, and no small Insight into the Devices of Satan. . . . She is well acquainted with . . . our Method of leading Souls; having gone thro' all our little Offices, and discharg'd them all entirely well. She has a ready utterance, a Spirit of convincing as well as of persuasive Speech: A winning Address, an agreeable Carriage, in whatever Company she is engaged. By means of all which she is exceedingly beloved, almost wherever she comes, and is dear, in an uncommon degree, to great numbers of the People.

'And as to the Fruits of her Labours, I never yet heard or read of any woman so own'd of God: So many have been convinc'd of Sin by her private Conversation: And so many have received Remission of Sins in her Bands or Classes or under her Prayers. I particularly insist upon this. If ever I have a Wife, she ought to be the most usefull Woman in the Kingdom: Not barely one, who probably *may* be so (I could not be content to run such a hazard) but one that undeniably is so. Now, shew me the Woman in England, Wales or Ireland, who has already done so much good as G[race] M[urray]. I will say more. Shew me one in all the English Annals, whom God has employ'd in so high a degree? I might say, In all the History of the Church, from the Death of our Lord to this day. This is no Hyperbole, but plain, demonstrable fact. And, if it be, who is so proper to be my Wife?

'I cannot doubt but such a person being constantly with me (for she is both willing and able to accompany me in all my Journeys . . .) would be so far from being an hindrance, that she would remove many Hindrances out of the way. She would, in great measure, either prevent or remove, those bodily Weaknesses and Disorders, which now increase fast upon me. By caring for me, she would free me from a thousand cares, and enable me to serve God with less Distraction. She is and would be a continual Defence (under God) against unholy Desires and inordinate Affections: Which I never did entirely conquer, for six Months together, before my intercourse with her. . . .

'But she would not only remove Hindrances. Such a Friend and Fellow-labourer (I do not say probably would, but actually does) greatly assists and furthers me in my Work; inlivening my dull and

K

dead Affections, composing and calming my hurried thoughts, sweetning my Spirits, when I am rough and harsh, and convincing me of what is true, or persuading me to what is right, when perhaps no other cou'd. At the same time, loosening my Soul from all below, and raising it up to God.

'She would likewise remove many Hindrances from others, from Women in particular. She would guard many from inordinate Affection for me, to which they would be far less expos'd, both because they would have far less Hope of Success, and because I should converse far more sparingly with them. Perhaps not in private with any Young Women at all; at least not with any Member of our own Societies.

'And she might directly further the Work, by employing all her Grace and Gifts on that very thing: In regulating Female Classes and Bands: in examining, instructing, reproving, comforting: In awakening Souls (under God), bringing them to the Faith and building them up therein.

'Therefore all my Seven Arguments against Marriage, are totally set aside. Nay, some of them seem to prove, both that I ought to marry, and that G[race] M[urray] is the Person.'

Has any woman ever been more closely analysed by the one who loved her? And could any clergyman's wife get a finer testimonial?

The moment they returned from Ireland to Bristol, Grace heard rumours that Wesley was interested in another woman, and in a fit of jealousy she wrote to John Bennet. The next day she regretted her impulsive action and confessed it to Wesley, but the letter had already been sent, and soon he received a momentous letter from John Bennet. It seemed that marriage between Wesley and Grace Murray was not thought desirable by the Methodists, and she was advised most earnestly to refuse to marry Wesley, lest she should be the cause of destroying all the work of God that was in his hands. Wesley and Grace travelled northwards and in Epworth Wesley and Bennet had a talk which persuaded Wesley that it would be better if Bennet married Grace. He wrote to tell her that they ought not to meet again, but Grace came to him in tears and Wesley allowed himself to be mollified. Again Grace was successful in convincing Wesley that she would marry him, but Wesley who later made the rule for his helpers, 'Take no steps towards marriage without first consulting with your brethren' felt it incumbent upon him to consult Charles, and of course to make known to Bennet the changed situation. His letter to Bennet did not arrive, but a copy of it reached the newly-married Charles in Bristol.

At this alarm, Charles saddled his horse and hastened north. John was not surprised to see his brother, and reported their discussion. 'The thought of my *marrying* at all, but especially of my marrying a

Servant, and one so *low-born*, appear'd above measure shocking to him. Thence he infer'd, That it wou'd appear so to all Mankind: and consequently, that it would break up all our Societies, and put a stop to the whole Work of God.' Charles was also considering the probable effect upon Bennet, and consequently upon the whole body of preachers.

The next day, unknown to John, Charles rode to the nearby village where Grace Murray was staying with some friends. Completely worn out by fatigue and nervous strain Charles met her with the words: 'Grace Murray! You have broken my heart!' and immediately fainted. When he came to himself again, he used all his powers of persuasion to get her to give up the marriage and showered her with reproaches, assuring her that his brother was of his own mind.

He left the perplexed and deeply troubled Grace and rode as fast as he could to Newcastle to get John Bennet to take Grace back. Not unnaturally Bennet had now become weary of all this disputation and refused to take Grace but Charles was intent on uniting them and rode back to fetch Grace and bring about a reconciliation.

While all this was going on Wesley had been attending to his work as usual. After speaking at Hindley Hill he returned to the little house where he expected to find Grace but discovered that his brother had been there two hours before and had taken her away with him. Wesley accepted this discovery with resignation. 'The Lord gave, and the Lord hath taken away: blessed be the name of the Lord.'

The owner of the house, however, was much distressed on Wesley's account and offered to travel to Newcastle to fetch Grace back. Wesley let him go. 'In a quarter of an hour, he took horse, and I calmly committed the Cause to God.'

The following day he devoted to prayer, fasting, and self-examination. 'I now closely examin'd myself touching what was so confidently laid to my charge, viz. Inordinate affection. And this I clearly perceived, That I had never before had so strong an Affection for any Person under Heaven. . . . I need add no more, than that if I had had more Regard for her I loved, than for the Work of God, I should now have gone on strait to Newcastle, and not back to Whitehaven.'

It was to Whitehaven, however, that he went through a storm that swept across the fells so that he had great difficulty in keeping on his horse. 'But I knew where help was to be found, in either great difficulties or small.'

The wedding of John Bennet and Grace Murray took place on the 3rd October 1749—eight days after Wesley had written down his elaborate reflections on Grace and marriage. Thus quickly had the whole thing happened. After the wedding, Grace, Bennet, and Charles rode off to Leeds to meet Wesley; he ironically analysed the purpose of this awkward encounter: 'As well that I might have the pleasure of seeing the Bride, as "that I might acknowledge my Sin" (those were my Brother's Expressions) before J[ohn] B[ennet] and them all. But this I was not altogether ready to do.'

Whitefield was also at Leeds and ready to do his part in bringing the two brothers together, and Wesley recorded in detail the next stage in the contention.

'I (Wesley) lay down by him (Whitefield) on the bed. He told me, "My brother would not come till J[ohn] B[ennet] and G[race] M[urray] were married." I was troubled. He perceived it. He wept and prayed over me, but I could not shed a tear. He said all that was in his power to comfort me, but it was in vain. He told me, "It was his judgement that she was my wife, and that he had said so to J[ohn] B[ennet]: that he would fain have persuaded them to wait, and not to marry till they had seen me; but that my brother's impetuosity prevailed and bore down all before it.

'I felt no murmuring thought, but deep distress. I accepted the just punishment of my manifold unfaithfulness and unfruitfulness, and therefore could not complain. But I felt the loss both to me and the people, which I did not expect could ever be repaired. I tried to sleep, but I tried in vain; for sleep was fled from my eyes. I was in a burning fever, and, more and more thoughts still crowding into my mind, I perceived if this continued long it would affect my senses. But God took that matter into His hand, giving me, on a sudden, sound and quiet sleep.

'Thurs[day] 5. About eight one came in from Newcastle, and told us, "They were married on Tuesday." My brother came an hour after. I felt no anger, yet I did not desire to see him. But Mr Whitefield constrained me. After a few words had passed, he accosted me with, "I renounce all intercourse with you, but what I would have with an heathen man or a publican." I felt little emotion. It was only adding a drop of water to a drowning man, yet I calmly accepted his renunciation and acquiesced therein. Poor Mr Whitefield and John Nelson burst into tears. They prayed, cried, and entreated, till the storm passed away. We could not speak, but only fell on each other's neck.

'J[ohn] B[ennet] then came in. Neither of us could speak, but we kissed each other and wept. Soon after I talked with my brother alone. He seemed utterly amazed. He clearly saw I was not what he thought, and now blamed her only; which confirmed me in believing my presage was true, and I should see her face no more.'

John Wesley and Grace Bennet were indeed to meet once again when both were advanced in age, a brief impersonal and unemotional greeting. Bennet broke with Wesley some time after his marriage, though his wife remained a Methodist. The reconciliation of the two brothers was genuine, two of John's comments upon it revealing his realism and his humility. 'I can forgive, but who can redress the wrong?' 'If I have any strength at all (and I have none but what I have *received*) it is in forgiving injuries.' Neither Charles's interference nor his own personal loss was allowed to spoil his single-minded obedience in the service of God.

Chapter XX

Wesley's Marriage

EARLY IN 1751, John Wesley was called to Oxford to vote in the Parliamentary elections. Although he did not find the University in the state he could have wished it, he could not help noticing a change in the attitude towards him: 'I was much surprised, wherever I went, at the civility of the people—gentlemen as well as others. There was no pointing, no calling of names, as once; no, nor even laughter. What can this mean? Am I become a servant of men? Or is the scandal of the Cross ceased?' He remembered the warning of Christ: 'Woe unto you, when all men shall speak well of you.'

This kindly treatment was a temptation to Wesley to return to the comfortable and secure life behind university walls, far from slander and abuse. Several years later he broke out: 'Let me be again an Oxford Methodist!' The trials and opposition he and his friends had experienced in the Holy Club were as nothing compared with the hostility he had met with later as an itinerant preacher. Within Methodism, however, the two brothers were loved and honoured and sometimes unwittingly became a focus for the attention of certain of the movement's women who found it hard to distinguish between the clergyman and the man.

Ten years earlier James Hutton had written to Count Zinzendorf: 'J[ohn] W[esley] and C[harles] W[esley], both of them are dangerous snares to many young women; several are in love with them.' Now Charles was married and was consequently scarcely a snare for anybody, but John was still free to marry or remain single. His straightforward attitude towards his fellows and his assumption that their motives were as unmixed as his own sometimes involved him in situations that a man more circumspect and worldly-wise would have been able to avoid. This fact explains a number of unnecessarily warm phrases in some of his letters to female correspondents.

A few of Wesley's friends among the clergy advised him to marry if he could find a middle-aged woman who was well situated and who had not previously been too actively connected with the Methodist societies. This in their opinion would mollify public opinion and strengthen public confidence in his work. Wesley himself gave his own reasons for marriage in his *Journal* 2nd February 1751. 'Having received a full answer from Mr [Vincent] P[erronet], I was clearly convinced that I ought to marry. For many years I remained single, because I believed I could be more useful in a single than in a married state. And I praise God, who enabled me so to do. I now as fully believed that in my present circumstances I might be more useful in a married state; into which upon this clear conviction, and by the advice of my friends, I entered a few days after.'

Old Samuel Wesley had once said about John that as a boy he would not even do the most natural things unless he could give clear and logical reasons for his actions. This trait of character he had preserved throughout his life, and at the age of forty-eight, having set on one side a marriage in which he might have given his heart, the evangelist, preacher, and leader of a great people's revival married because he was convinced that marriage would make his work for God more effective. His diary shows that he felt himself to be an exception to the general rule which he urged upon his preachers a few days before his marriage. 'Wednesday, 6 [Feb. 1751]. I met the single men, and showed them on how many accounts it was good for those who had received that gift from God to remain "single for the kingdom of heaven's sake"; unless where a particular case might be an exception to the general rule.'

Who then was this woman whom historians of Methodism have depicted in somewhat glaring colours, but who in a number of more recent biographies, particularly those written by women, has received more sympathetic treatment? Some have even gone to the opposite extreme and pictured Mrs Wesley as a misunderstood angel, while the great evangelist is represented as a man whose self-centred compulsion to work outstripped his capacity for domestic affection.

Mary Wesley's first marriage had been to a well-to-do London merchant called Vazeille by whom she had several children. When she married Wesley, he arranged for the whole of her fortune to be handed over to the children.

Wesley's first intimate contact with the widowed Mrs Vazeille was the result of a mishap. He had slipped and sprained his ankle on a bridge in London and some good friends carried him to Mrs Vazeille's home in Threadneedle Street so that she could attend to him.

Two other women had previously cared for Wesley during brief periods of sickness, Sophy Hopkey in Georgia and Grace Murray in Newcastle. On both occasions Wesley had felt the urge to marry his nurse, touched by her interest and care for his well-being. In a state of temporary dependence he found his needs supplied by the motherly care of Mrs Vazeille, and 'without first consulting with (his) brethren' he persuaded her to marry him on the 18th or 19th February 1751.

Charles was angry because his brother had not informed him about what was going on. On 2nd February he wrote in his diary: 'My brother, returned from Oxford, sent for and told me *he was resolved to marry!* I was thunderstruck, and could only answer, he had given me the first blow, and his marriage would come like the *coup de grâce*. Trusty Ned Perronet followed, and told me, the person was Mrs Vazeille! one of whom I never had the least suspicion. I refused his company to the chapel, and retired to mourn with my faithful Sally. I groaned all the day, and several following ones, under my own and the people's burden. I could eat no pleasant food, nor preach, nor rest, either by night or by day.'

During the ensuing days Charles was quite beside himself and found it difficult to be even civil to his new sister-in-law, whom he knew quite well already, as she had accompanied Charles and his wife on a journey of visits to the Methodist societies. From youth fiery and passionate, Charles was at this time suffering trials to his patience, at home two sisters-in-law had joined his family, and in the Methodist societies in London which were giving him trouble. But there was more than hasty exasperation in his reactions to his brother's proposals to Grace Murray in 1749 and to Mrs Vazeille in 1751. The whole of his life he had been filled with a unique and devoted admiration for his brother. No one knew better than Charles what John Wesley was really worth, and he was afraid lest he might impetuously take to himself someone who might weaken his influence or hamper his divine vocation.

It was far from Wesley's intention that his marriage should hinder him in his work. A few weeks after his marriage he wrote: 'I cannot understand how a Methodist preacher can answer it to God to preach one sermon or travel one day less in a married than in a single state. In this respect surely "it remaineth that they who have wives be as though they had none".'

As he taught, so he lived, but this did not mean that he felt no tenderness towards his wife. One of the first letters he wrote to her on his travels was written at Tetsworth, about fifty miles from London, and dated 27 March 1751:

'My dear Molly,

'Do I write too soon? Have not *you* above all the people in the world a right to hear from me as soon as possibly I can? You have surely a right to every proof of love I can give and to all the little help which is in my power. For you have given me even your own self. O how can we praise God enough for making us helps meet for each other! I am utterly astonished at His goodness. Let not only our lips but our lives show forth His praise! . . .

'If any letter comes to you directed to the Rev. Mr John Wesley, open it: it is for yourself. Dear love, adieu!'

This was no youthful, passionate love-letter, it is true, but it was written by a man of some forty-eight years, and the gentle tenderness he expressed was certainly genuinely felt.

Not more than three days elapsed before he wrote again.

'My dear Love,

'Methinks it is a long, long time since I wrote to you. So it seems, because while I am writing I see you before me: I can imagine that I am sitting just by you.'

For her part Mrs Wesley was undoubtedly in love with this man, and she did her best to give happiness to this strange person who had obviously had only one great passion in the whole of his life: to win souls for God and His Kingdom. She herself had no education and the religious dissertations her husband wrote were as wearisome and irrelevant for her as were her little domestic problems for him.

The greatest literary light of the age, Samuel Johnson, was on one occasion presented to Wesley and a deep and far-ranging discussion was begun, but was brought to an end too soon for Johnson because Wesley would not allow conversation to usurp the place of duty. 'John Wesley's conversation is good,' he told Boswell, 'but he is never at leisure. He is always obliged to go at a certain hour. This is very disagreeable to a man who loves to fold his legs and have out his talk, as I do.' The gift of releasing himself in everyday conversation was denied to John Wesley whose conscience bound him to use every moment as one who would have to give an account.

Her husband resisted the temptations of domestic ease so Mrs Wesley fell in with his wishes and accompanied him on his travels round the country. Leaving her quiet and comfortable home, she lived through riots, street-fighting and stonings, she journeyed along muddy highways and snow-covered tracks, spent the night in filthy inns, served with food that was offensive to her housewifely instincts. She made an honest attempt to keep pace with this bundle of energy that she had taken as husband, but eventually it became too much for her.

As time went on the difficulties increased and in a letter to one of his friends Wesley expressed his dissatisfaction with his wife who had been with him on his last tour of the North but was now back again in London.

'In my last journey into the North, all my patience was put to the proof again and again; and all my endeavours to please, yet without success. In my present journey I leap as broke from chains. I am content with whatever entertainment I meet with, and my companions are always in good humour "because they are with me". This must be the spirit of all who take journeys with me. If a dinner ill dressed, or hard bed, a poor room, a shower of rain, or a dusty road will put them out of humour, it lays a burthen upon me greater than all the rest put together. By the grace of God I never fret, I repine at nothing, I am discontented with nothing. And to hear persons at my ear fretting and murmuring at every thing is like tearing the flesh off my bones.'

The relationship was no longer that of nurse and patient. Wesley was no longer in his sick-room, but labouring in God's great harvest field, where no person or thing must hinder him in his work.

Mrs Wesley with her narrow domestic background never really succeeded in understanding her husband and did not realize that the devotion which she craved had been partly stifled by her own complaints and importunities. Affectionate he could indeed be to her, but any friendliness he showed to other women aroused in her a jealousy that gradually became pathological and found a quite grotesque outlet.

Certain of the letters written by Wesley to his female colleagues or to people seeking his advice in spiritual matters had an affectionate tone and in Mrs Wesley's imagination assurances of devotion and esteem became veritable declarations of love. Jealousy and spite drove her to make piquant additions to the letters which she handed over to Wesley's worst opponents at this time, the Calvinists, who triumphantly published these stolen and distorted private letters in their own journal.

By his very naïveté Wesley himself also put weapons in the hands of his enemies. A woman with trigamy on her conscience who had repented and been converted, was made housekeeper of the Methodist homes in Bristol and Kingswood by John Wesley who often quoted her as an example of what the grace of God could achieve. He wrote to her in this appreciative strain. 'The conversing with you, either by speaking or writing, is an unspeakable blessing to me. I cannot think of you without thinking of God. . . . You bring me straight into His presence.' He made the more serious mistake of writing to her about his domestic problems, and this naturally aroused the resentment of his wife who when Wesley publicly testified to the beneficial influence Mrs Ryan had had on his Christian life, did not hesitate to give her own version of Mrs Ryan's character.

Wesley hoped to moderate his wife's outbursts and besought her in a letter to endeavour to be 'a private, insignificant person, known and loved by God and me. . . . Leave me to be governed by God and my conscience. Then shall I govern you with gentle sway and show that I do indeed love you even as Christ the Church.' This position of submissiveness Mrs Wesley was not prepared to accept.

The relationship between them gradually became bizarre. John Hampson, one of Wesley's preachers who had a grudge against Wesley and later deserted him, wrote of a lamentable scene he had witnessed.

'I was once on the point of committing murder. Once, when I was in the north of Ireland, I went into a room, and found Mrs Wesley foaming with fury. Her husband was on the floor, where she had been trailing him by the hair of his head; and she herself was still holding in her hand venerable locks which she had plucked up by the roots. I felt as though I could have knocked the soul out of her.'

Mrs Wesley broke open her husband's desk and stole his letters and parts of his diary that were not yet published, and in 1771 she deserted her husband. This is the short entry we find in the *Journal:* 'Wednesday, 23 (Jan. 1771). 'For what cause I know not to this day—set out for Newcastle, purposing "never to return". *Non eam reliqui; non dimisi non revocabo!*' ['I have not left her; I have not sent her away; I will not recall her.'] This was about the time when she was delivering Wesley's correspondence to his Calvinist enemies, who published them in their magazine in a distorted form, so that purely spiritual expressions appeared to be the expression of physical passion.

A little while later, however, Mrs Wesley made it known that she was more than willing to return to him. Wesley answered her thus:

'Things standing thus, if I was to receive you just now without any acknowledgement or reparation of these wrongs, it would be esteemed by all reasonable men a confirmation of all you have said.

'But it may be asked, "What reparation are you either able or willing to make?"

'I know not if you are willing to make any. If you are, what reparation are you able to make? Very little indeed; for the water is spilt, and cannot be gathered up again.

'All you can do now, if you are ever so willing, is to unsay what you have said. For instance, you have said over and over that I have lived in adultery these twenty years. Do you believe this, or do you not? If you do, how can you think of living with such a monster? If you do not, give it me under your hand. Is not this the least you can do?'

So far as we know there was never any answer to this letter, and the last record of Mrs Wesley is in the diary dated Friday, 12th October 1781: 'I came to London, and was informed that my wife died on Monday. This evening she was buried, though I was not informed of it till a day or two after.'

This was, then, the end of the marriage that had been one great misunderstanding all along and that had created grief and despair not only for the two people directly involved but also for Wesley's many friends.

Wesley himself felt that perhaps there might have been a providential purpose in all this so that he might throw himself into his work as an evangelist free from the temptations of a comfortable home life.

Cutting himself loose from Grace Murray, becoming involved in a hopelessly unpromising marriage with a woman whom John Telford called 'one of the worst wives of whom we have ever read', Wesley showed himself to be ill-adapted for this relationship. His real marriage was to his work and in this he never faltered.

Chapter XXI

The Organizer

METHODIST SOCIETIES were now growing up with surprising speed throughout the whole of England. They were forced to expand their organization farther and to seek help from other clergymen and from lay helpers. By 1744 Wesley had acquired some fifty 'lay assistants' who travelled round the circuits to which he appointed them, preaching and building up the societies. At the start of the revival Wesley adhered staunchly to this 'principle of necessity'. His primary aim was to get the clergy to interest themselves in the newly-converted, but when they were hostile or indifferent, he had to get help wherever he could.

During the early days Wesley had had all the work under his own control, but in 1744 he summoned some preachers to a Conference at the Foundery so that various questions connected with preaching and practice among the Methodists might be discussed and the responsibility to some extent shared with others.

The first annual Conference consisted of six clergymen of the Anglican Church and four of Wesley's lay preachers. On the evening of the 24th June 1744, they attended Holy Communion together and the next morning Charles preached to the assembled brethren. Then the objects of the Conference and the spirit in which they met were contemplated; one of the resolutions reads: 'It is desired that all things may be considered in the immediate presence of God; That we may meet with a single eye, and as little children who have everything to learn; That every point may be examined from the foundation; That every person may speak freely whatever is in his heart.' They also posed this question: 'How far does each of us agree to submit to the unanimous judgement of the rest? . . . In speculative things each can only submit so far as his judgement shall be convinced: in every practical point so far as we can without wounding our consciences.'

Then the Conference passed on to the business of the day. There were three questions on the agenda: '1. What to teach; 2. How to teach, etc.; 3. What to do, i.e., how to regulate our Doctrine, Discipline, and Practice.' Wesley laid great stress on the doctrines of justification, sanctification, and the witness of the Spirit. They did not feel called upon to formulate any new doctrine, nor did they try, but they placed renewed emphasis on that part of the common Christian faith that dealt with practical Christian living, and which had been seriously neglected.

How then should they preach? The best methods of preaching are '1. To invite. 2. To convince. 3. Offer Christ. And lastly to build up. And to do this (in some measure) in every sermon.'

As early as this Conference they had to decide upon their attitude towards the Established Church. It was made clear in the invitations to the Conference that there was no thought of forming any new Church, but that questions relevant to the revival would be discussed. The dichotomy in Wesley's view of the Church emerged straightaway in his reply to this question: 'How far is it our duty to obey the Bishops?' The answer was: 'In all things indifferent. And on this ground of obeying them, we should observe the canons, so far as we can with a safe conscience.' This was a wise and far-sighted formulation of policy by a man who would have liked to work within the framework of the Church, but who was, nevertheless, driven ever farther away from it. Wesley remained a member of the Church of England to the end of his life.

The Minutes of the Conference also give us an interesting glimpse of how Methodism was organized in 1744. The question reads: 'How are the people divided who desire to be under your care?' 'Into the United Societies, the Bands, the Select Societies, and the Penitents.' 'How do these differ from each other?' 'The United Societies (which are the largest of all) consist of awakened persons. Part of these, who are supposed to have remission of sins, are more closely united in the Bands. Those in the Bands, who seem to walk in the light of God, compose the Select Societies. Those of them who have made shipwreck of the faith, meet apart as penitents.'

Definite rules for each one of these four divisions were decided upon. Among the rules for the United Societies we find among other things: 'There is one only condition previously required in those who desire admission into these societies—a desire "to flee from the wrath to come, to be saved from their sins". But, wherever this is really fixed in the soul, it will be shown by its fruits.' Then the rules enumerate actions that Methodists should abstain from, and the good deeds that a Methodist ought to concentrate on in order to gain grace. In the third place it is strongly emphasized that Methodists shall diligently employ all means of winning grace.

This strict division of Methodism into societies, classes, bands, and select societies did not last for ever, for Wesley's 'bands' were intended to be a form of Protestant confessional where the members could acknowledge their sins to one another and seek the forgiveness of God, but it soon became apparent that not every such circle had the wisdom and reliability needed by those who receive the confidences of their fellow-members.

The same thing can be said even more truly of Wesley's 'Select Societies', whose very name sounded boastful. Actually, those who joined were genuinely conscious of their own sinfulness, but they had before their eyes a good which they longed for—perfect love to God and men. Some of their number with great meekness and inward thanks to God bore witness that God had already granted them this experience.

It sometimes happened that some of these claimants to Christian perfection fell from grace or showed by their behaviour that there was still a long way to go before they were full of love alone, and the 'Select Societies' lost their quality, much to Wesley's disappointment. When it came to the point, it was clear that neither the 'bands' nor the 'Select Societies' had the right to live and they therefore faded out, mostly in Wesley's life-time, and today they are not found at all in Methodism.

It was quite different with the class-meeting, which satisfied the need of its members for fellowship and personal activity. Here they brought their sorrows and joys, here they sang Charles Wesley's hymns and searched the Scriptures. Here they could introduce their neighbours to the Lord, and bring their offerings towards His work. All this gave them a blessed sense of *belonging*.

Wesley expected the Methodists to observe Holy Communion in the parish churches and attend the other services there. In Wesley's day no Methodist meetings were held at the times of the Anglican service, and this custom persisted in many places long after his death. It was Wesley's wish that the Methodists should form an active and zealous organization within the Anglican Church.

Wesley entertained a warm affection for his preachers. They had left their trades and businesses to go out into the work of God's vineyard, and Wesley made himself personally answerable for their well-being. He took charge of their education, issuing books to help them in their studies and advising them to devote several hours a day to reading. He collected his preachers together on courses in which he delivered lectures to them as he had once done at Oxford. In 1753 he assembled seventeen of them at Kingswood and lectured them on the tenets of their faith, logic, and the rules of delivery and clear pronunciation. He was prepared too, to point out their limitations; to one of his preachers he wrote: 'Abstain from controversy—indeed you have not a talent for it. You have an honest heart, but not a clear head.'

To another who was intoxicated with his own progress, he wrote: 'I think you tasted of the powers of the world to come thirteen or fourteen years ago, and was then simple of heart, and willing to spend and be spent for Christ. But not long after, not being sufficiently on your guard, you suffered loss by being applauded. This revived and increased your natural vanity; which was the harder to be checked because of your constitutional stubbornness;—two deadly enemies which have lain in wait for you many years, and have given you many deep, if not mortal, wounds.'

He disassociates himself in rather pungent terms from the 'evangelist preachers' of his time: 'I find more profit in sermons on either good tempers, or good works, than in what are vulgarly called Gospel sermons. That term has now become a mere cant word: I wish none of our society would use it. It has no determinate meaning. Let but a pert, self-sufficient animal, that has neither sense nor grace, bawl out something about Christ, or his blood, or justification by faith, and his hearers cry out, "What a fine Gospel sermon!" Surely the Methodists have not so learned Christ!'

Wesley disliked shouting or theatrical preachers. His men were expected to deliver what they had on their minds in a quiet, rational, and heartfelt manner.

They were also expected to be continually on the move. 'I have too great an interest in my preachers' bodies and souls to allow them to confine their labours to one place.' He felt that even he would find himself lulling a congregation to sleep after preaching to them for a year. When membership of one of the societies went down in one year from one hundred and sixty to about fifty, Wesley thought he knew the reason. 'Such is the fruit of a single preacher's staying a whole year in one place!'

Wesley's preachers, then, had to be always on the move, and to go where Wesley appointed them. To Francis Wolfe, who should have been in Bristol but who for one reason or another had failed to arrive there at the time appointed by Wesley, he wrote this short but expressive epistle: 'Franky, are you out of your wits? Why are you not at Bristol?'

The ideal of poverty that Wesley followed in his own personal life, he considered ought also to apply to his preachers. He relates with obvious admiration how he once on a highway met 'John Jane, who had set out on foot from Bristol with three shillings in his pocket. Six nights out of the seven since he set out he had been entertained by utter strangers. He went by us, we could not tell how, and reached Holyhead on Sunday with one penny left.' The same preacher left little behind him at his death. 'All his clothes, linen and woollen, stockings, hat, and wig, are not thought sufficient to answer his funeral expenses, which amount to one pound seventeen shillings and threepence. All the money he had was one shilling and fourpence. . . . Enough for any unmarried preacher of the gospel to leave to his executors.'

Wesley provided for the preachers' keep mostly from the collection that was taken weekly by the class-leaders, but also from the sale of his own writings. There was no collection at Methodist meetings. 'No preacher connected with me begs for money—either directly or indirectly.'

He was very strict in matters concerning the preachers' personal life and behaviour. He who could strike out large numbers of members of the societies throughout the land if it was proved they had fallen from grace, might also take a strong line of action with preachers who had failed him in some sphere or other.

He was by no means lacking in sympathy but showed real compassion with those who had fallen from grace. Perhaps the most beautiful testimony to this is the letter Wesley wrote to the Methodist society in Keighley in 1779. It concerned the former barber and Methodist preacher, William Shent, who had fallen into sin:

'London, January 11, 1779.

'I have a few questions which I desire may be proposed to the Society at Keighley.

'Who was the occasion of the Methodist preachers first setting foot in Leeds? William Shent.

'Who received John Nelson into his house at his first coming thither? William Shent.

'Who was it that invited me and received me when I came? William Shent.

'Who was it that stood by me while I preached in the street with stones flying on every side? William Shent.

'Who was it that bore the storm of persecution for the whole town and stemmed it at the peril of his life? William Shent.

'Whose word did God bless for many years in an eminent manner? William Shent's.

'By whom were many children now in paradise begotten in the Lord and many now alive? William Shent.

'Who is he that is ready now to be broken up and turned into the street? William Shent.

'And does nobody care for this? William Shent fell into sin and was publicly expelled the Society; but must he be also starved? Must he with his grey hairs and all his children be without a place to lay his head? Can you suffer this? O tell it not in Gath! Where is gratitude? Where is compassion? Where is Christianity? Where is humanity? Where is concern for the cause of God? Who is a wise man among you? Who is concerned for the gospel? Who has put on bowels of mercy? Let him arise and exert himself in this matter. You here all arise as one man and roll away the reproach. Let us set him on his feet once more. It may save both him and his family. But what we do, let it be done quickly.

'I am, dear brethren,
'Your affectionate brother,
'John Wesley.'

This handsome testimony of Wesley's love for those who had shared an evangelist's work with him also explains the intimate devotion the preachers felt towards him, so that they would go through fire and water for him.

Here lies the deepest secret of Wesley's great success as an organizer: he was no theorist who explained to others how they should behave; he himself shared the lives of his friends with his whole heart.

Chapter XXII

Homo Unius Libri

IT IS SAID of Wesley that he wrote two hundred and thirty original works of which some were indeed very original! Green's bibliography of works bearing Wesley's name contains no less than four hundred and seventeen items, but in it are included all the works that Wesley abridged or edited and published in his own name.

Wesley made a great contribution towards popular culture in England merely by creating a completely new class of reader. People who had been preoccupied with the doubtful pleasures of the time felt on their conversion an urge to read about the new life that had opened before them.

Now that they no longer frequented public houses, they were relatively well off. Gin cost money, both directly when they were actually paying for it and indirectly because those who drank it became less fitted for work. Now they had got other interests they had the means to purchase a small tract for a penny or a little book by Wesley—a portion of his *Journal* for example—for sixpence. This was the first step along the path of culture.

These tracts and books were written in vigorous everyday English, such as any ordinary man could understand; their appetite grew with reading, and Wesley worked immensely hard to satisfy this new need. He led people a step at a time along a path of reading that was safe and sure. He wanted them to read books that 'dealt with God and led to a knowledge of God'. The work of grace would be destroyed if the preaching of the Word were not supplemented by these pamphlets and books, which were either written or approved by himself. The censorship which he exercised had in it no suggestion of bigotry; his motto was: 'We think and let think.' But his preachers were 'unlearned and ignorant men', and when they left the shoemaker's stool or the stonemason's quarry to spend much of the day in prayer and study, it was only too easy to wander at random over the oceans of knowledge if they lacked supervision. They might well have distorted the gospel, giving weight to unimportant things and leading their hearers astray.

It was inevitable that a few should fall into the trap of the half-educated: conceited arrogance and narrow-mindedness. Charles saw this danger more clearly than John, and wrote bitingly to a friend of his: 'A Friend of ours [i.e. his brother] . . . made a Preacher of a Taylor.

I with God's help, shall make a Taylor of him again.' But John, too, knew how to write to self-important friends in such a pungent and at the same time affectionate manner that the balloon of conceit was quickly pricked.

For the most part the preachers found great happiness in the new world of reading which Wesley made available for them, and some of them even managed to become experts on classical languages, history, and first and foremost, the Bible.

The Bible was for Wesley the source of all wisdom. The preface to one of his collections of sermons reads: 'To candid, reasonable men, I am not afraid to lay open what have been the inmost thoughts of my heart. I have thought, I am a creature of a day, passing through life as an arrow through the air. I am a spirit come from God, and returning to God: Just hovering over the great gulf; till, a few moments hence, I am no more seen: I drop into an unchangeable eternity! I want to know one thing—the way to heaven; how to land safe on that happy shore. God himself has condescended to teach the way: For this very end he came from heaven. He hath written it down in a book. O give me that book! At any price, give me the book of God! I have it: Here is knowledge enough for me. Let me be *homo unius libri*. Here then I am, far from the busy ways of men. I sit down alone; Only God is here. In his presence I open, I read his book; for this end, to find the way to heaven. Is there a doubt concerning the meaning of what I read? Does anything appear dark or intricate? I lift up my heart to the Father of Lights: "Lord, is it not thy word, 'If any man lack wisdom, let him ask of God?' " '

This 'man of one book' nevertheless read books of all ages and by all sorts of authors. When Charles and he were walking from Oxford to Epworth as impecunious students, they formed the habit of walking in single file with the one at the back reading aloud to the one in front. John's constant concern was to use every minute to good purpose and many were the books he read on horseback, in carriages, and in village inns. Notes about some of these books are to be found in his *Journal*.

'In riding to Newcastle I finished the tenth *Iliad* of Homer. What an amazing genius had this man, to write with such strength of thought and beauty of expression, when he had none to go before him! And what a vein of piety runs through his whole work, in spite of his Pagan prejudices! Yet one cannot but observe such improprieties intermixed as are shocking to the last degree.'

'In riding to Cirencester I read Dr Bates's *Elenchus Motuum nuperorum in Anglia*. His Latin is not much inferior to Caesar's whom he seems studiously to imitate.'

Wesley read some of the works of the Swedish Baron Emanuel

Swedenborg and assessed both the weaknesses and the strength of that contemporary philosopher:

'He is one of the most ingenious, lively, entertaining madmen that ever set pen to paper.'

'It surely contains many excellent things. Yet I cannot but think the fever he had twenty years ago, when he supposes he was "introduced into the society of angels", really introduced him into the society of lunatics; but still there is something noble, even in his ravings.'

About Watts's *Doctrine of the Passions*, he says dryly and laconically: 'His hundred and seventy-seven pages will make a useful tract of four-and-twenty.'

Among Wesley's belongings was found a well-used copy of Shakespeare's works in which Wesley had written marginal comments. Shakespeare was not as popular in eighteenth-century England as he is today; his wide range of emotions and characters were not valued by an age that set great store by the classical conventions. Wesley, however, read him with close attention and interest and it is regrettable that one of Wesley's close friends thought he would do his memory a service by burning this book which would certainly have thrown a revealing light upon Wesley's character.

His intention in his reading was not merely to enrich his own mind, but to find suitable material which he could publish, recommend, or even, perhaps, warn against. Time after time we see his forefinger raised in admonition or in guidance. To a young woman Methodist with whom he often exchanged letters in later years, he suggested: 'By confining yourself to those who write clearly your understanding will be opened and strengthened far more than by reading a multiplicity of authors.'

The first book Wesley himself published was a collection of prayers which appeared as early as 1733, while he was in Georgia. Here he published, too, the book *Imitation of Christ* and in 1737 a hymn-book.

He permitted himself a fairly large measure of freedom in his treatment of original texts. In 1768 he wrote: 'In the latter end of the month I took some pains in reading over Dr Young's *Night Thoughts*, leaving out the indifferent lines, correcting many of the rest, and explaining the hard words, in order to make that noble work more useful to all, and more intelligible to ordinary readers.'

There were no laws of copyright at this time, and corrections were taken as a matter of course. Even plagiarism and piracy passed uncensored, luckily for Wesley. But his intentions were always to supply his people with the best possible reading matter, and no one in his opinion was better qualified to provide this than John Wesley himself! Whatever the subject, his purpose was the same. 'My view in writing history (as in writing philosophy) is to bring God into it.'

Wesley was also drawn into the field of polemic writings as Methodism was attacked from all sides. The chief opponents were the High Anglicans, and a controversy with Bishop Lavington lasted for more than two years. In addition he was attacked by Calvinists both within the Methodist movement and outside. He was attacked by his own friends, the Moravians, and by many others who frequently misunderstood Methodist doctrine and practice.

Religious controversy for Wesley was 'heavy work, such as I should never choose; but sometimes it must be done'. He did it objectively, briefly, and pointedly. But he was soon to find that his opponents did not follow the same rules for exchange of views. 'Oh that I might dispute with no man! But if I must dispute, let it be with men of sense.'

Wesley also wrote a number of tracts: *A Word to a Sabbath-Breaker*, *A Word to a Drunkard*, *A Word to a Smuggler*, which were all published at a penny each.

Between the years 1746 to 1760 Wesley published forty-four sermons which had a wide sale. Together with his *Explanatory Notes upon the New Testament* these sermons constituted the Methodist standard of doctrine. A second series of sermons came out in 1788, and the last sermon Wesley wrote appeared in 1790. It is called 'The Wedding Garment' and was written a year before he himself was called to the great wedding feast.

In his *Explanatory Notes upon the New Testament* that came out in 1755 Wesley gave his preachers, and all other Methodists, a short and concise commentary which he himself described as 'plain truth for plain people'. He did not discuss alternative interpretations but stated his own convictions. The text of the Bible itself was heavily drawn upon but the work was not too bulky to be carried in a preacher's saddle-bag.

Wesley translated thirty-three hymns from German, one from Spanish and one from French. He had a strong poetic vein, but could not as a rule rise to the heights of the genius of Charles who enriched English hymnody with over seven thousand hymns.

Wesley also published the *Arminian Magazine*, a gold-mine for anyone who wishes to study early Methodism. He called the magazine 'Arminian' because he was a follower of the Dutch theologian Arminius who taught that salvation could be received by all, as opposed to the Calvinist tenet that some were pre-destined to be saved and some to be damned. Later the journal was re-named the *Methodist Magazine*.

For use in his schools Wesley wrote and published a large English dictionary and grammars of Hebrew, Greek, and Latin.

In his *Primitive Physick* he criticized medical practices of the age and advocated the use of simple remedies and the practice of hygiene. He was also a pioneer in the use of electrical treatment.

In his 'Christian Library' in fifty volumes Wesley published selections from Christian literature from the Christian Fathers up to his own time. It was an economic venture of some magnitude and he lost money over the affair. Later on, however, he discovered that he was on the way to becoming rich by his authorship, but he devoted the proceeds of his literary work to the salaries of preachers, and charitable gifts.

Of particular interest are Wesley's many letters. They comprise eight large octavo volumes and reveal much about the man himself and his work. Somebody who knew Wesley personally could testify that 'He wrote as he spoke. Their [i.e. the letters'] unstudied simplicity must give this impression; and I myself who often heard him speak, can attest its justness . . . [He] literally *talks* upon paper.'

The simple clarity of the style is so distinctive that it has been claimed that if only a fragment of Wesley's letters is read to intelligent English-speaking Methodists, they will cry out: 'This is John Wesley!'

The Wesley scholar Henry Bett re-wrote a short extract from John Wesley in the style used by Joseph Addison and Samuel Johnson respectively. It is like going from a clean, practical, and plain room to rooms filled with all kinds of bric-à-brac. There was no stylistic window-dressing or flowery rhetoric in Wesley. Here was plain, direct, and powerful English, a man who 'spoke on paper'.

He himself discussed the question of style in this way:

' "What is it that constitutes *a good style?*" Perspicuity and purity, propriety, strength, and easiness, joined together. . . . As for me, I never think of my style at all; but just set down the words that come first. . . . When I had been a member of the University about ten years, I wrote and talked much as you do now. But when I talked to plain people in the Castle or the town, I observed they gaped and stared. This quickly obliged me to alter my style and adopt the language of those I spoke to. And yet there is a dignity in this simplicity, which is not disagreeable to those of the highest rank.'

He wrote on another occasion: 'I dare no more write in a *fine style* than wear a fine coat.'

Even his shortest letters were full of matter. One of the briefest he ever wrote was to one of the preachers, informing of his new appointment: 'Dear Simon, You shall be in Oxfordshire. Adieu.'

By means of letters he administered the steadily growing Methodist Connexion, arranged his itineraries, transferred his preachers, answered questions about affairs in the societies, and attended to the building of chapels. Many of his letters were of a pastoral nature and showed his unique knowledge of people. He remembered people he had not met for years, and he knew all his preachers through and through. He could discipline and chastise, he was as forgiving and loving as his Master towards the repentant. The overwhelming content of his correspondence comprised exhortations and promptings to continue the fight for the gospel.

In his later years Wesley took particular joy in exchanging letters with a couple of young women Methodists. They were people who had gone whole-heartedly into the work of Methodism and the old wanderer without family or domestic happiness poured out his fatherly warmth upon these young people.

The last letter but one which Wesley wrote was to William Wilberforce, who fought against negro slavery with such zeal and fortitude. Wesley encouraged him thus: 'But if God be for you, who can be against you? Are all of them together stronger than God? O be not weary of well doing! Go on, in the name of God and in the power of His might, till even American slavery (the vilest that ever saw the sun) shall vanish away before it.'

His *Letters*, his *Journal* and various publications show Wesley's quality as a writer. He was at the same time a man of one book and a man of many books; he brought his wide reading upon many subjects into the service of God and encouraged his preachers and members of society to do the same.

Chapter XXIII

Onward

'Here lieth the Body
of
JOHN WESLEY
A Brand plucked out of the burning:
Who died of a consumption in the fifty-first year of his age,
Not leaving, after his debts are paid,
ten pounds behind him:
praying
God be Merciful to me, an unprofitable servant!'

THIS WAS not exactly how the epitaph on John Wesley's grave finally read, but it is the inscription that he himself ordered to be inscribed on his tombstone if he had departed at the age of fifty-one, as once seemed likely. He composed the text himself, so that well-meaning admirers would not crown his last resting-place with 'vile panegyric'.

Wesley believed at the time that he had tuberculosis and felt himself getting weaker every day. He retired to the home of one of his friends to die. After an illness of more than a year, his recovery was effected by the waters of a hot spring near Bristol, and he was soon as active as before.

During his period of sickness he was still busily occupied. It was then he wrote his *Explanatory Notes on the New Testament*—a work he would scarcely have attempted had he 'not been so ill as not to be able to travel or preach, and yet so well as to be able to read and write'.

It was certainly of great importance that Wesley should get well again, for Methodist societies were spreading at an ever-increasing rate and John now had less help from his brother Charles. When John fell ill, Charles went to London to take over his brother's work, but he soon found that the burden of the work was too heavy for him.

Charles had married in 1749 and in 1756 he retired from itinerant activity. His state of health and his family ties pointed towards this decision, and it was also clear that his judgement and his brother's did not always coincide. Charles was an unusually gifted preacher with particular power of appealing to people to take an immediate decision for God. He feared no danger and spared no effort in evangelism, but organization was not his strong point.

From 1756 until his death Charles participated in the work of the two great Methodist centres, London and Bristol. Here he preached and administered the sacraments and with his prayers and sermons he seemed to bring Heaven itself into the place of meeting. He was loyal to John if he did not always agree with him, and was able to tell him so quite frankly. But when on one occasion he received a letter from a leading Calvinist Methodist, the aristocratic Lady Huntingdon, who enclosed a printed attack on John, he endorsed the letter: 'Lady Huntingdon's last. Unanswered by John Wesley's brother!'

In 1757 Wesley found a new and valued colleague in John Fletcher. Born in Switzerland in 1729, Fletcher came to England in 1752 and soon got a position as a private tutor. In London he happened to hear of the Methodists and soon afterwards joined the Methodist society in West Street. On the advice of John Wesley he sought and received ordination in the English Church and from then on became one of Wesley's closest collaborators and dearest friends.

Fletcher came into Wesley's life like an answer to prayer. He had prayed for God's help in holding Holy Communion in the London Chapels, where he often had about six hundred communicants on Sundays. To officiate at such a crowded Communion was, in Wesley's opinion, 'equal to preaching eight times'. Now the newly-ordained Fletcher came to help him and Wesley exclaimed 'How wonderful are the ways of God! When my bodily strength failed, and none in England were able and willing to assist me, He sent me help from the mountains of Switzerland, and an helpmeet for me in every respect. Where could I have found such another?'

Fletcher was called 'the saint of Methodism'. As a parish minister in Madeley, where he later settled down, he exercised a powerful and beneficial influence over his congregation and the town. When he started to write, he was a figure to be reckoned with throughout the land, and next to Wesley himself became Methodism's best apologist. He was according to the view of the age 'one of the best polemists any Church has ever fostered'. He wrote with German thoroughness and French clarity, and he added to these qualities a goodly measure of practical English common sense, and all these qualities he placed at the disposal of God. Isaac Taylor says of him: The Methodism of Fletcher was Christianity, as little lowered by admixture of human infirmity as we may hope to find it anywhere.'

It was expected that Fletcher would take over the leadership of Methodism after Wesley, and he was known as 'Methodism's Crown Prince', but by 1785 he had died, six years before Wesley.

At the same time that Wesley received this valuable addition to his company of preachers, he was having difficulty with many of the others. Worst of all were those who thought they had attained 'entire sanctification'. Wesley insisted that he had more difficulties with them in six months than he had in years with other preachers who laid no claim to experience.

Among those who broke away from Wesley about this time was Thomas Maxfield, the first layman to preach in the Foundery. He gathered together several hundred members and formed his own society. Another of the preachers prophesied that the world would come to an end on 28th February 1763, and when this did not happen, he lost his faith.

But in spite of many problems and set-backs, Wesley's flock of preachers was a strongly-welded group of men who under vigorous leadership became a blessing to many, and enjoyed a warm sense of fellowship among themselves.

At the Annual Conference held in 1770 Methodism was divided up into fifty 'circuits'. One of these 'circuits' was America! Round about 1770 there were some hundred members in New York, and four ministers preached the Word of God up and down the American colonies. The beginnings of Methodism in America and its subsequent remarkable development is an unusually interesting chapter in Church history, though it is not possible to say more about it here.

Gradually the ranks of the first generation of Methodist preachers began to thin out. In 1770 George Whitefield died in America. To the last, he preached God's Word with great power and enthusiasm and he was gladdened by the success of the orphanage Bethesda in Savannah. He was due to hold a meeting one morning in Newburyport, but already the evening before people had begun to collect in large crowds outside the house where he was living as they had heard that he was coming, and wanted him to preach then and there. But Whitefield felt tired and worn-out. 'Brother,' he said to a clergyman who was present, 'you must speak to these dear people; I cannot say a word.' Then he took a candle to make his way upstairs to his room. But on the stairs he stopped; he could not resist the longing of the crowd who had gathered to hear him. He spoke to them and went on speaking until the light he held in his hand burned down and went out.

He awoke in the small hours with a serious attack of asthma, and at six in the morning he entered the land of perpetual light.

Wesley and Whitefield had agreed that the one who lived the longer should preach the funeral sermon for the other, and it was Wesley who thus commemorated his old colleague.

About this time a new conflict with the Moravians arose, and in 1770 it proved necessary to clarify the Methodist position once again on the issue of salvation by works. Wesley comments on the statement that ' "a man is to do nothing in order to justification". Nothing can be more false. Whoever desires to find favour with God should "cease from evil, and learn to do well". Whoever repents should do "works meet for repentance". And if this is not in order to find favour, what does he do them for? . . . Is not this salvation by works? Not by the *merit* of works, but by works as a *condition*.'

The minutes in which these statements appeared were for the use of Wesley's preachers. Antinomianism, the doctrine that Christians are exonerated from the obligations of the law, had spread like an epidemic among Methodist societies, and it was very necessary to stop the rot.

The Calvinist branch of Methodism, too, was creating problems for Wesley at this time. Lady Huntingdon strongly censured Wesley and the Conference but finally made an apology.

Far worse were the more bigoted Calvinists, such as the hymn-writer Toplady and some of his helpers, who for nine years attacked Wesley in their newspapers and pamphlets. They called him 'the lying Apostle of the Foundery', 'a designing Wolf', 'a dealer in stolen wares', and many more such epithets and made common cause with the jealous and scheming Mrs Wesley. Wesley, however, carried on serenely as though nothing had happened. He had promised to take his young niece Sally, one of Charles's daughters, with him on a journey to Canterbury, on the very day that his letters had been published in garbled form. Charles begged him not to go, as it might bear the appearance of flight. John had no such qualms: the journey had been decided upon. 'When I devoted to God my ease, my time, my fortune, my life, did I except my reputation? No. Tell Sally I will take her to Canterbury tomorrow.'

Wesley found himself able to meet opposition and controversy with courage but two illnesses made it nececessary for him to come to a decision about the leadership of Methodism after he had gone. In 1774 and 1775 Wesley was several times at the threshold of death, and newspapers even went so far as to announce that he was dead. Again pressure was brought to bear on Charles to take over his brother's position, but fortunately it turned out that Wesley recovered again and was able to carry on his task with undiminished strength for the next ten years. Near to death in a severe attack of influenza he wrote:

'I have been wandering up and down between fifty and sixty years, endeavouring, in my poor way, to do a little good to my fellow-creatures; and now it is probable that there are but a few steps between me and death; and what have I to trust to for salvation? I can see nothing that I have done or suffered that will bear looking at. I have no other plea than this:

I the chief of sinners am,
But Jesus died for me.'

The work in London was crying out for new premises to take the place of the Foundery which was now too small and unworthy of the steadily growing movement. On the 1st November 1778, City Road Chapel was opened, a building in Wesley's words, 'perfectly neat, but not fine; and contains far more people than the Foundery: . . . Many were afraid that the multitudes, crowding from all parts, would have occasioned much disturbance. But they were happily disappointed; there was none at all. All was quietness, decency, and order. I preached on part of Solomon's prayer at the dedication of the Temple.'

To begin with only ordained ministers were permitted to preach there. They read prayers every morning and evening in accordance with Anglican practice and administered the sacraments. Later on it became usual for Wesley's lay preachers also to preach God's word in 'the Cathedral of Methodism'.

In the house next to the chapel lived Wesley and those preachers who were stationed in London. Here Wesley died and in the graveyard he rests with a large number of his preachers and other followers, in the grounds nearby.

In 1776 there were 3,184 members in America; by 1784 the total was exactly 12,914—and the number increased rapidly. Francis Asbury was called 'the John Wesley of America' as he travelled round America for fifty-five years as Wesley did in England. Every day he read a hundred pages and devoted three hours to private prayer.

It was necessary to make sure that all these people received the Sacrament of the Lord's Supper. Wesley asked the Bishop of London if one of his preachers might be ordained so that the numerous believers in America might receive the benefit of Communion. The strange reply was that there were already three ministers in that country. And that was that!

After the American colonies had declared their independence of England in 1776, several of the Methodist preachers returned home and Asbury consequently needed more help. Wesley examined this question in the light of the Bible and Church history and soon came to the conclusion that presbyters and bishops were of one and the same 'order'. No new ordination was required for a presbyter to become a bishop, but only consecration. Wesley was himself a presbyter by virtue of his ordination, and believed it permissible that he should ordain preachers who could administer the sacraments wherever circumstances should require. Together with another Anglican clergyman he ordained Dr Coke to supervise the work in America and gave him the title of Superintendent. Together with Wesley the newly-appointed Superintendent then ordained two additional preachers so that they could administer the sacraments.

Charles strongly protested against these ordinations which seemed to him to indicate disloyalty to the principles of the Established Church and to be a usurpation of episcopal rights. But once the decision was taken John Wesley would not yield; devotion to God's cause always weighed heavier with him than formal obedience to statutes or conventions. In the following year he ordained three 'well-tried' preachers to administer Communion in Scotland.

The authority for nominating and stationing preachers was invested in Wesley himself as were the rights of ownership of the many Methodist chapels that had sprung up throughout Great Britain. When Wesley fell ill, it was time to start planning for the future. In 1784, therefore, Wesley issued 'The Deed of Declaration'. It was registered with the authorities in the same year. In it Wesley laid down that after his death, the right to nominate preachers should fall to Charles Wesley. Upon the death of Charles this responsibility should pass to the Annual Conference which was to consist of one hundred itinerant preachers, men nominated by Wesley himself, the Legal Hundred, a number to be permanently maintained. There were at this time more than two hundred preachers in Great Britain, and many felt themselves slighted because they had not been chosen.

In spite of differences of outlook and policy John and Charles Wesley were closely united to one another in spirit the whole of their lives. Their friendship dated from the years they spent together in their childhood home in Epworth. It was strengthened at Oxford, put to the test and deepened in Georgia, welded together in the fire of revival and trial. Now as old age approached it was a great happiness for Wesley that his brother moved from Bristol to London and the brothers could occasionally meet and maintain contact with one another.

On 29th March 1788, Charles Wesley died. At the moment that he was fighting his last battle, John was at a meeting in the Midlands where they sang Charles's famous hymn:

> 'Come, let us join our friends above
> That have obtained the prize.'

Delay in the post prevented John from attending his brother's funeral which took place in St Marylebone churchyard in London. He had been unwilling to be buried in a Methodist burying-ground because it was not consecrated by the Church. Side by side with Charles rest his wife and two sons, who were both organists and outstanding musicians. One of them adopted the Catholic faith. They had inherited their father's musical temperament, but were completely opposed to Methodism's message and way of life.

Some time later Wesley was addressing a meeting in Bolton. They were singing his brother's hymn 'Wrestling Jacob'. When they came to the lines:

> 'My company before is gone
> And I am left alone with Thee,'

Wesley in an outburst of sudden realization of loss broke down and wept. The hymn drew to a close and the whole assembly shared the sorrow of the solitary patriarch who must now carry on his fight alone a little longer until he was called himself to join his friends above.

Chapter XXIV

Journey's End

THE GATHERING years were taking their toll, yet in his own eyes and in the eyes of others Wesley was still a strong, healthy person. The only thing that really troubled him was that he was receiving so many marks of honour. Towns that only a few decades ago had persecuted him, now received him with remarkable affection. 'Do I yet please men?' Wesley asked himself. 'Is the offence of the Cross ceased?'

At the age of eighty-two he wrote wonderingly: 'Is anything too hard for God? It is now eleven years since I have felt any such thing as weariness. Many times I speak till my voice fails, and I can speak no longer; frequently I walk till my strength fails, and I can walk no farther; yet even then I feel no sensation of weariness, but am perfectly easy from head to foot. I dare not impute this to natural causes; it is the will of God.'

It may be added that he was helped by his ability to relax and lay down all his troubles so that they would not disturb his sleep or over-strain his powers.

A year later he wrote: 'I am a wonder to myself. . . . I am never tired (such is the goodness of God!), either with writing, preaching, or travelling. One natural cause undoubtedly is my continual exercise and change of air. How the latter contributes to health I know not, but certainly it does.'

When Wesley was eighty-four, he began to realize that he was not quite so active as before, and could not jump out of bed with his former alacrity. His sight was weaker, too, and he had continual headache as the result of a fall. He found it difficult to remember names and numbers he had just heard, but those he had heard or seen thirty or forty years before were not so difficult to remember. But—'Nor do I feel any such thing as weariness, either in travelling or preaching; and I am not conscious of any decay in writing sermons, which I do as readily, and, I believe, as correctly, as ever.'

In the interests of truth it should be said that others were more conscious of Wesley's infirmities than he was himself. He was quite capable, for example, of remaining asleep until midday—something that would have been quite unthinkable a few years earlier.

He never preached more than twice a day now, and usually refrained from preaching at five o'clock in the morning.

In 1790 the following entry in his *Journal* is in a shaky handwriting that is scarcely legible: 'For upwards of eighty-six years I have kept my accounts exactly. I will not attempt it any longer, being satisfied with the continual conviction that I save all I can, and give all I can, that is, all I have.'

His last letter to America was written in 1791. It was very important to him that Methodists should live as one people the whole world over. Those who now wished to write to him or had anything on their minds would now have to express it very soon, for time had said farewell to him and death was not far away.

When Wesley walked through the streets he was greeted respectfully by everyone he met. He answered by quoting his favourite text: 'Little children, love one another!' And in every assembly he visited he repeated the exhortation: 'Love the brotherhood. Fear God. Honour the King.'

It was Wesley's constant prayer that he would not live so long that he would be useless. In 1791 he still wished to travel to the North upon his usual journey, but it never materialized. On the 17th February, he preached in Lambeth, and his last sermon of all was preached in a private house on the text: 'Seek ye the Lord while He may be found; call ye upon Him while He is near.'

The next day Wesley was brought home to City Road to die. He sat down in his room and asked to be left alone for half an hour. Then he was put to bed in a high fever and with uneven pulse. For several days he was very ill, but managed to get on to his feet and appeared to be improving. During his illness he said over and over again some lines from one of his brother's hymns:

'I the chief of sinners am,
But Jesus died for me!'

and repeated, 'we must be justified by faith, and then go on to sanctification. There is no way into the holiest but by the blood of Jesus'.

He asked for pen and ink to write something down, but felt himself too weak to hold the pen. 'Let me write for you, sir,' said one of his friends, 'tell me what you would say.' 'Nothing, but that God is with us.'

He bade those who stood round him to praise God and pray. As they left him after the prayer, he said farewell to each of one them, and lifted his voice with the assurance, 'The best of all is, God is with us!' Raising his arms as a sign of victory he repeated in a weak voice: 'The best of all is, God is with us!' Mrs Charles Wesley came to visit him and he broke out into the prayer of thanks he used to use after meals: 'We thank Thee, O Lord, for these and all Thy mercies; bless the Church and King: grant us truth and peace, through Jesus Christ our Lord for ever and ever!'

A few minutes before ten o'clock next morning, 2nd March 1791, John Wesley died. The last word they heard from his lips was 'Farewell!'

The day before the funeral his coffin was laid near the entrance to City Road Chapel so that the throngs of people could pass by him. He lay there with a peaceful and celestial smile on his face. It has been estimated that some 10,000 people passed in front of the coffin, and it was thought best to close the grave when few were present, and the burial was therefore arranged for six o'clock in the morning. This became known the evening before, and thousands of people attended the simple rite.

Six poor men received twenty shillings each to carry Wesley to his grave. On the gravestone stand the words: 'This great light arose (by the singular providence of God) to enlighten these nations. Reader, if thou art constrained to bless the instrument, give God the glory.'

At his death Wesley left behind nothing more than the right to his books. They were bequeathed to the Methodists to further their work.

When Wesley died there were three hundred and thirteen preachers in Great Britain and seventy-six thousand nine hundred and sixty-eight members. In America there were one hundred and ninety-eight preachers and fifty-seven thousand six hundred and twenty-one members.

And throughout the world are still to be found people both within and outside Methodism who think with love and reverence about the spare, little man of God who once used to ride through the towns and villages of England and now travels farther and farther into the minds and thoughts of men each succeeding day.

INDEX

Index